To Ka
What c

10%

an
HONEST
house

Cynthia Reyes
May 2016

Let me not pray to be sheltered from dangers
but to be fearless in facing them.
Let me not beg for the stilling of my pain
but for the heart to conquer it.

~ Rabindranath Tagore

an HONEST house

A MEMOIR, CONTINUED

CYNTHIA REYES

BPS books

www.bpsbooks.com

Published in 2016 by
BPS Books
Toronto
www.bpsbooks.com
A division of Bastian Publishing Services Ltd.

ISBN 978-1-77236-036-3 (paperback)
ISBN 978-1-77236-037-0 (ePDF)
ISBN 978-1-77236-038-7 (ePUB)

Cataloguing-in-Publication Data available from
Library and Archives Canada.

 Canada Council   Conseil des arts
for the Arts   du Canada

The author gratefully acknowledges the Canada Council
for the Arts for its support in the writing of this book.

Editors: Lesley Marcovich and Donald Bastian
Cover painting: Stephanie MacKendrick
Author photo: Edward Gajdel
Cover design: Daniel Crack, Kinetics Design
Text design and typesetting: Kinetics Design, kdbooks.ca

To Hamlin and our family,
with thanks for your love, faith, and courage.
And to the memory of Aunt Rose,
who insisted on a second book.

Contents

Part One   Where the Lawn Breaks

One	Ambercroft	3
Two	Gone	6
Three	The House	13
Four	The Promise of Spring	19
Five	A Visit with Dr. Helen	23
Six	My Church Throws a Party	30
Seven	An Oath of Cowardice	35
Eight	A Call from Aunt Rose	39
Nine	Tuesdays with Sarah	43
Ten	My Family	51
Eleven	Our Neighbours	57
Twelve	The Library	64
Thirteen	The Fountain Pen	72
Fourteen	My Tightrope, a Bridge	77
Fifteen	Kicking Pain in the Teeth	81
Sixteen	Looking PTSD in the Eye	85

Part Two   Taking to the Verandah

Seventeen	Sharing the Harvest	89
Eighteen	The Matriarch and the Uncle	94
Nineteen	Each Season Brings a Gift	104

Twenty	A Precious Hour	108
Twenty-one	Mighty Dawson	113
Twenty-two	Home for Christmas	118
Twenty-three	In Bed with a Dead Poet	123
Twenty-four	Angels	126
Twenty-five	The Mysterious Valentine Card	130
Twenty-six	Friends	132
Twenty-seven	Lent and Borrowed	140
Twenty-eight	A Job That Pays	145
Twenty-nine	No More Calls from Paddy	148
Thirty	Lorna's Prayer	154
Thirty-one	Spring Fever	159
Thirty-two	How Hard Could It Be?	165
Thirty-three	Courage in Its Different Forms	173
Thirty-four	Running Away to Home	182
Thirty-five	The Return to Dr. Helen	191

Part Three   A Stream Runs Through It

Thirty-six	A Tough Act to Follow	201
Thirty-seven	A Good Man	204
Thirty-eight	It's Always Something	208
Thirty-nine	Hamlin the Undercover Cop	212

Forty	Hamlin's Perfect Birthday	222
Forty-one	Sunshine and Clouds	225
Forty-two	The Test of a Man	231
Forty-three	Tea with Shelagh	233
Forty-four	Hamlin's Sudden Turn	235
Forty-five	Hamlin's Comeback	247
Forty-six	In This Together	253
Forty-seven	The Things We Do Not Know	255
Forty-eight	Hamlin's Revelation	260
Forty-nine	Out with the Snow Warriors	265
Fifty	Making Advent Count	268
Fifty-one	A Quieter Christmas	272
Fifty-two	Farewell to the Farmhouse	277
	Acknowledgements	283
	About Post-Traumatic Stress Disorder	285
	Resources	295
	Discussion Questions for *An Honest House*	298

Part One

Where the Lawn Breaks

Chapter One

Ambercroft

"Ambercroft Farm," the sign out front said.

Hamlin was on a first-name basis with the grand old farmhouse right from the start, calling it Ambercroft. For years, I didn't call it anything at all.

The tall, two-storey Victorian house on the northern edge of Toronto seemed sealed off from the rest of the neighbourhood. Within a solid wooden fence and gates, massive maples waved big leafy arms. Pines and dense blue-green spruces soared. A cedar hedge ran the length of the property on one side.

This was a private place, sure of its personality and power.

~

I had loved our former home east of the city, the small Blue House in the woods we had moved to in the 1990s. But I never forgot the first time I saw it at the end of a long country lane: I wanted to drive away without looking inside, without even walking the grounds. A plain, flat-roofed house, a too-modern house, it had not piqued my interest, much less tugged at my heart.

And yet, it was a home in which we became happy,

even content. It was as if it had pulled us there, knowing it was what we needed at that time in our family's life.

Through the huge windows in almost every room, we experienced sunlight and moonlight and star-filled night skies. Inside it, I often felt I was standing in the woods, the walls and windows my second skin.

In fact, when I think of the Blue House now, it is not the structure itself that I remember most. It is living in the woods; it is the gardens, the meadow, and the comforting sound of the small stream splashing and gurgling as it made its way downhill.

And I remember how powerful I felt, heaving rocks to build a long stone wall in front of the house, digging to build a new garden bed, hauling thick branches from the woodlands for the new rustic pergola that Hamlin was building.

It had been such a good home. A place of joys and contentment, creativity and growth.

Then, after nearly a decade of living there, it was time to move on. The thought had slapped me in the face like an insult.

"We can't remain children in the woods forever," I told Hamlin. "One of these days we'll have to move to something more adult, a grown-up house."

Without realizing it, we had done a lot of growing up in the Blue House. So had the consulting company Hamlin and I had created in this home. Now, in late 2004, our business, almost five years old, was ready to expand. We needed to move closer to the city. We figured we had fifteen good working years ahead of us to recoup large outlays of money spent on establishing the business, our children's education, our elder daughter's wedding.

~

The stately red brick farmhouse answered practical needs, yes. It was closer to the city, to our relatives, clients, and friends. It had enough rooms for our family, and two offices that were perfect for working from home, which we often liked to do.

But as we stared at the large living room with elegantly carved fireplace mantel, the library with panelled walls and floor-to-ceiling bookcases, the dining room with fabric-clad walls and large windows, our hearts skipped a beat.

We saw, in our minds, wreaths hanging on doors, garlands on the staircase banister, and candles on the beautiful fireplace mantel. Our whole family agreed it was a "Christmas house."

"We can finally have a tall Christmas tree!" our daughters said.

With twelve-foot ceilings? Yes, we could.

We marvelled at the tall mullioned windows, the deep millwork around windows and doorways, the handsome, soaring maple staircase and gleaming wooden floors. Even the bedroom ceilings upstairs were tall.

The Blue House was small and made of wood. Instead of feeling protected by it, I felt protective toward it. This farmhouse was very different, with a foundation made of huge field stones, walls made of three layers of brick outside, plaster inside, and, heavy wooden doors.

"Built to protect its inhabitants from danger," I whispered to Hamlin.

The tour over, we looked at each other and nodded. It was time. Time to leave the woods. Time to get serious about our lives and our work.

Chapter Two

Gone

How serious, we were soon to discover.

Two weeks before our move, a car crashed into mine on a dark country highway.

My whole body seethed with pain. I seemed to be living in a permanent daze. But no blood had been spilled. I took solace in this fact and tried to reassure my loved ones in the months that followed.

"I'll get over this," I told my daughters, when just taking a deep breath made me wince.

"I'll be okay. Really, I will," I told Hamlin, as he studied me, eyes narrowed over my frequent inability to hold a thought and express it clearly.

"It's only a matter of time," I said to my sister, whose keen eyes and ears seemed to fasten on every one of my grimaces and sighs.

Months later, I returned to work, glad to be part of a team again. I took on only one project, the kind of work I loved. With a full partner assigned to work with me and the help of the team, I felt privileged. Best of all, this project required only a few days' work a week, giving me time for physiotherapy, rest, and visits to doctors.

I should have realized that the willpower and perseverance that had won me awards for achievements in career and community work would not be enough. But I refused to even countenance the thought.

"It's only a matter of time," I told Hamlin and other team members, repeating the mantra even as I returned to spending more and more days in bed and speaking became more difficult. Lack of sleep at night was taking its toll on my days.

Time passed. The injuries didn't.

It took me nearly two years to face it: instead of recovering, I was getting worse. Alone in the house one day, I admitted to a series of stark truths.

Easy mobility? Gone.

Independence? Gone.

Eloquent speech, quick wit, easy confidence? Gone, gone, gone.

The ever-present painkillers, the hours at physiotherapy, and the many days spent lying down should have made me better. But the pain never left, varying only in its severity.

And something even more frightening lurked in the shadows – something for which I had no name but that often struck without warning.

Our beautiful grown-up house was becoming my prison.

~

I would have liked to come to this house whole and well, my own strong and sure self. To be able to stand up straight and look the house in the eye and at least fool myself into thinking that we were equals, meeting each other on our own terms.

I would have liked to say: "You're the house; I'm the human. We each have a role to play in this relationship.

I will take care of you – clean you, repair you, pay the bills. You will stand firm, sheltering my family from cold and wind and sun and rain."

But it wasn't that kind of relationship.

Night after night, unable to sleep because of pain, unwilling to sleep because of nightmares, I argued with the house, yelled at it, even swore at it. Night after night, I lay awake, silently quarrelling with the house and with God about the injustice of it all.

And when neither of them answered, I raged even more.

~

There were moments of clarity over the next few years. Each time what I called a clear day arrived, I persuaded Hamlin to let me work again. Torn between the trouble of having to work closely with me and his desire to help me recover, he reluctantly agreed.

Inevitably, I'd start to fade within two days, but on that first clear day, I was always sure I had returned from the dark for good.

I had been a journalist, editor, executive producer of a network television series, trainer, and consultant. I had used my writing and public speaking skills in all of those roles. Now, I often spoke with a stutter, it sometimes took me an hour to compose a short email, and I was afraid to speak in public.

Sleep was perilous. I would awaken and try to shake the terrors of the night, failing every time. I was convinced that I was in the grip of Alzheimer's disease.

I often did not speak, except to silently yell at the walls of the bedroom around me. Even thinking was a challenge. I was ashamed to answer the phone and terrified to walk out the door.

If forced to communicate during those times, I used a

desperate mixture of made-up sign language and strange assortments of words, leaving my family to guess what I was trying to say.

The headaches that followed my attempts were vicious. Exhausted, I returned to my bed, turned my face to the wall, and gave up. I stopped writing for long periods. The effort was too great.

~

Strangely enough, it was a doctor who helped me start writing again. Dr. Helen, my specialist at one of Canada's most famous hospitals, was patient and kind, but her first direction was unsettling.

"Write," she said.

I stared back at her.

"Write," she repeated. "It's the only way anyone will understand you. There aren't many specialists who have two hours to decipher what you're trying to say. But ... you used to be a writer, didn't you? So write. Write how you're feeling every day. What challenges you have. Where it hurts. And come back and see me with what you've written."

Those were not her exact words, of course. I often forgot events minutes after they happened. But something about this woman made me want to do what she asked, or at least to try.

So I bought a journal – and promptly misplaced it. Searched and searched, gave up and got a second – only to misplace it, too. Bought a third, but left it downstairs on days when pain trapped me upstairs.

It took me months to figure out the solution: putting a journal or notebook in every room of the house, including the bathroom, and on the front verandah and back verandah, too. I was determined to follow the doctor's order.

Here and there, daytime and nighttime, I wrote. In phrases, single words, and short sentences, I wrote about the pain I lived with; about the times when I felt entirely lost in a thick mist of confusion; about having lost the will to live. In longer sentences, I wrote about the rare moments when I realized – with a shock of joy – that I was thinking clearly. I couldn't believe I had thought of dying, I told my journal; I wanted this clear day to never end.

But of course it did end. So, in tortured handwriting, I described the frustration of being trapped; the moments when I felt myself sliding back down into the pit of pain and confusion, with no strength to stop my fall.

And I wrote about the farmhouse.

First, as my captor. The house had quietly become my whole world. I knew all its corners, all its edges, and had resigned myself to staying within its limits.

Much later, it would become something else.

Years after moving here, I would have precious moments in which I saw the house clearly, as if for the first time. Precious moments in which I felt surges of gratitude: for our sheltering home, for my family and friends, for life itself. I would scribble, hurriedly, before the thoughts went away.

Unknown to me, the journals would become important later.

⁓

Also unknown to me, I would come to love the house – fiercely.

I finally grew to understand it: its rhythms, sounds, silence. I learned about its ancestry from visitors who had lived here earlier, and from descendants of the people who had built the house in the 1860s.

I wrote about these things in my journals.

It was also here in this house, five years after we moved

in, that Hamlin would begin his search for the stories I had written across twenty-five years of a high-flying creative life, most of it in network television.

"Here's another," he'd say as he found them. "You must read this."

These were the personal stories, the ones I had put away and forgotten when we moved to the farmhouse. Many had been written on airplanes, in hotel rooms, and once even on a train from Nova Scotia in the middle of a snow storm. All of them, one way or another, were about the many houses I had lived in and the people and experiences that accompanied them.

How was I to know that the stories my husband handed me, along with journals I had written in this house, would coalesce into a book and one day push me outside the front door, across the lawn, through the sturdy wooden gate, and into the world?

Sure, I had written, directed, and produced countless stories throughout my career. I had won awards for my earlier work in journalism, for the long-running television series I later produced, and for my role as a leader in the media industry. I had even been lauded for contributions to community and country.

But those honours were lost in the shadows of my former life. I had been stripped of worth and confidence and even my glorious past. On many days, I no longer believed I had ever been capable of such achievements.

And now I had visions of becoming an author?

I, who rarely left home, would do book readings in front of other people? I, who suffered pain whether standing or sitting, would stand and talk to an audience? I, who often stuttered and couldn't hold on to a thought – never mind speak in whole sentences – would answer questions about the book and sound intelligent?

You may as well have asked me to fly to the moon.

Yet, slowly, painfully, across two years, with the help of a dedicated group of relatives and friends, one therapist, two doctors, three editors, and one publisher – the book took shape.

It was like digging a diamond out of rock. With my bare fingernails.

Finally, in the early spring of 2013, the time had come. And when I had to choose a title for the book, I finally settled on the one that even a year earlier would have been unthinkable, after everything I had been through in this house.

I called it *A Good Home*.

Chapter Three

The House

While some modern dwellings pretend to be castles, this house was what it seemed: a spacious, well-built Ontario farmhouse.

Built in the 1860s, a time of great hope for the new country of Canada, it had been a good home for five families: two generations of farmers; one gentleman farmer after a high-profile public career; a prominent horseman who used the land and barns for his riding school; and a business executive and his wife and four children.

Thomas and Margaret, the Scottish immigrants who established it and passed it on to their son and his family, began by putting up a small wooden structure, circa 1860. A few years later, they added a larger storey-and-a-half brick building right next to it. Then came the pièce de résistance: the tall two-storey brick addition that gave the house its grandeur, completed in 1870.

By the time we first saw the house, the small wooden structure was gone, as were two large barns that had stood there for a century. Most of the land had been sold, as well.

Each family had maintained the house well and made some improvements. As the twentieth century progressed, pipes were put in to run water to the kitchen and bathrooms, and electrical lights were added. In time, the verandah was widened, the bathrooms and kitchen updated. Even then, the designs chosen were sympathetic. Beyond these changes, no one had dared make major alterations to the house. I think they respected it too much to do that.

~

Okay, I admit it: every once in a while I thought about making some major improvements. Like a really nice kitchen.

I drooled at the pictures of modern farmhouse kitchens in magazines: the creamy-white cupboards, the shiny stone counters.

"Wouldn't you like more counter space and deep pot drawers?" I asked Hamlin one day as he cooked dinner.

He raised his eyebrows and smiled.

"How about a really big island?" I continued. "I could be your sous-chef, peeling and cutting up vegetables over there at the island, while you do – whatever it is that gourmet chefs do."

Hamlin grinned and made a face. "I don't think I'd trust you with a knife," he said. "You could hurt yourself."

We laughed, knowing that renovations were unaffordable luxuries. I hadn't held a paying job in several years, despite enthusiastic – and short-lived – efforts to work.

Hamlin and I had gone from having two incomes to only one, relying now on his alone to pay all the bills, including some of my expenses for therapy and pain remedies. Frugality had been forced on us, but we were determined to live within its rules.

For one thing, I had learned that you don't need a fancy kitchen to make a good meal. I flashed back to the delicious meals my mother produced in my family's small, boxy kitchen in Jamaica. It had a modest fridge and stove, a few brown wooden cupboards under the sink, and very little counter space.

I could hear myself asking her, "How can you cook in this cramped little kitchen?" And hear her answer: "A bad workman blames his tools."

I often recalled how my mother had run her own household, and the tales I'd been told about the farmhouse by the grandson of its original owners, on his yearly visits to his old family home.

~

The farmhouse had been built for a large family – most farm families had been big – but the farm did not earn a big income during Bert's time here. Bert's family had grown or raised almost everything they ate, made the clothes they wore, and lived simply.

It seemed that we were repeating some of that pattern.

Hamlin tended his vegetable and herb garden every year. We learned to use everything the overall garden produced: the herbs, the vegetables, the fruit. From asparagus, spinach, chives, and Swiss chard in the spring to the abundant produce of summer and late fall. Apples, potatoes, onions, garlic, and beets all lasted well into the winter, rounding out many a meal.

My culinary skills were negligible, but I was good at a few simple things. Vegetable peel became stock for soups and gravy. I made jelly from our own apples – flavoured with mint from the herb garden – and from the red currant berries that grew on vigorous bushes in the side yard.

Hamlin made apple and pear pies and froze them; I roasted tomatoes in the oven and kept them in jars to use with fish, chicken, egg, and vegetable dishes. We made a variety of herb oils, using tarragon, sage, and basil from the garden. Olive oil infused with fresh basil and garlic made a delicious dressing for salads and cooked dishes alike.

We loved cooking with this oil. Small bottles of it also made good gifts for family and friends, as did jars of the jelly I made.

～

And our furniture? We never considered changing it, even if we could have afforded to do so.

The evidence of the old, the well used, and the completely out of fashion may explain why visitors described our home as "comfortable" and "honest."

There was nothing fancy, nothing "precious" – nothing that had a chance of ending up being photographed for its exquisite style. You rarely saw this kind of furniture in the pages of home decor magazines.

The plain-looking chest of drawers in one bedroom was made from butternut, the armoire in the living room from pine.

The harvest table in the kitchen was made of maple wood, the chairs from oak.

The timeworn pine chest in our bedroom bore an exterior that only someone drawn to primitive furniture could love. Our family may have been among the last in Canada to value and even respect this kind of simple Canadian furniture. After all, most of it had survived for more than a century.

And yet, despite our frugal habits and modest furnishings, despite a lack of frills and fripperies, the house retained an old-world elegance rarely seen anymore. High ceilings, wide transoms over doorways, and tall, mullioned windows will do that for a place.

～

On a wintry evening when the ground outside was covered by thick, fluffy snow, the electric lamps were turned off, and the only light in the living room came from flames leaping inside the fireplace, I imagined an earlier time of gentle lighting: the glow of candlelight, the flickering of lanterns.

The house was built at a time when doors and door-ways, fireplace mantels and crown mouldings around windows and ceilings, were made from strong, dense old-growth wood. Everything fit together as a united whole: the strong lines and sturdiness, the thick wooden mouldings, the tall windows and soaring walls.

Sometimes I stood in the living room and stopped to imagine the couple who had first lived here. The ambitions they must have had when they built this grand house.

Sometimes I ran my hands along the thick, meticulously crafted woodwork, and stopped to wonder about the artist-carpenters whose work stood true more than a hundred years later.

The beauty here was understated, timeless, and some of it was visible only to the heart. The rooms did not shout "look at me." Instead, they spoke in soft but assured voices, welcoming a visitor to stay awhile.

The living and dining rooms, the small library – all were of comfortable proportions. Not so small as to make one feel claustrophobic and not so large as to require shouting to make conversation.

The pine armoire containing some of my homespun blankets and woollen throws took pride of place in the living room. The maple harvest table stood comfortably on the wooden floors of the kitchen. In the library were two simple brown leather chairs, ideal for resting or reading.

Simplicity, rusticity, and quiet elegance. It was a harmonious blend.

~

Here in the farmhouse, I felt myself revelling in the smell and feel of freshly washed white cotton sheets. They felt luxurious, even though they had been used so many times.

Memories of my own childhood home tumbled through the years: bedsheets hanging from a clothesline, fluttering in the Caribbean sunshine and breeze. In my mind, I stopped to touch the sheets, to hold a corner against my face, to breathe in its freshness.

The privilege of living in a sturdy house, mixed with the small gifts of daily life, was mine. The blessing of sharing my life with the man I loved – and who knew me and loved me still in spite of everything – was mine.

Chapter Four

The Promise of Spring

It was only 4:57 a.m., but the orchestra was already in full swing. Between the twittering and the trilling, the cooing and the cawing, it was our very own symphony.

Every bird a musician. Right below our bedroom window.

Several weeks from now, I would be begging them – robins, cardinals, and countless others – to find another venue for their performance. A few weeks after that, I would mutter, pillow pressed against my ears: "Shut up, shut up! I need to sleep!"

But not now.

On this morning in the spring of 2013, after a long, harsh Canadian winter, this concert was a glorious wakeup call. I got up quietly so as not to waken my husband.

I smiled at the birds' noisy songs as I dressed, smiled as I slowly descended the farmhouse stairs. In this great old house with its thick walls, I could no longer hear them, but the sweetness of their songs carried me all the way through the hall to the kitchen, where I paused to make myself a mug of coffee.

In the mudroom, I opened the closet door and reached for my navy blue wool coat. The poor thing had suffered for being my favourite: it was so worn it had faded to a strange shade of purple.

"You need a new spring coat," Hamlin observed every time he saw me wearing it.

I always smiled, not bothering to remind him that the new one, the one I had bought several years earlier, was still tucked away in the far reaches of the closet, hardly worn because I rarely ventured past the edge of our lawn. Nor did I tell him this worn-out coat was still perfect for a walk in a damp spring garden.

I opened the door and, coffee mug in one hand, a cane in the other, crept outside into the loving kindness of spring.

"Thank you!" I told the air, the trees, the birds.

"Thank you!" I told God.

I was sure they were all smiling back.

~

I rounded the side of the house and walked toward Mama's Garden, named by Hamlin for my garden-loving mother who had died several years before.

The spring bulbs were blooming. The first of the tulips – large patches of them – glowed in luminous shades of pink. The last of the giant King Alfred daffodils nodded frilly yellow faces. The purple and yellow crocuses had flowered already, but the dead-nettle bloomed a fresh pink wherever it spread, sharing ground-cover space at the front of the garden with flowering clumps of sky-blue forget-me-nots.

All around me, leaves were unfurling, flowers were blooming or getting ready to bloom. Birds were singing, squirrels were chasing one another across the lawn, and the air was fresh and clean.

~

Twenty-three trees grew near the fence lines: maples, pines, spruce, cherry wood, and two old Wolf River apple trees. The trees towered over sprawling mature shrubs: burning bush, pink beauty bush, cream dogwood, red weigela, yellow forsythia, purple lilac, and a pure white bridal-wreath spirea.

I liked their names, their fragrance, the way they looked when in bloom.

These trees and shrubs provided a haven for the birds and squirrels in all seasons, and, in warm weather, for the bees and butterflies that flitted about. It was clear that this home didn't belong to us alone. So we provided seeds for the birds, grew butterfly-friendly flowers and shrubs, and welcomed the bees.

In late spring, we walked cautiously through the side yard, well aware that, in passing the robins' nest, we risked being dive bombed by an overprotective mother bird.

In autumn, we shared the apples with the squirrels. Not that we had a choice: the clever animals always set up house right near their food supply – in the apple trees. Still, we acknowledged, there were plenty enough apples to go around.

But saints we were not. When our garden was invaded by a whole family of wild rabbits, I wanted to wring their lovely necks. Pretty to look at, with fawn-coloured fur, fluffy white tails, long ears, and limpid eyes, the rabbits were merciless thieves. They were especially fond of the lettuce and snow peas my husband planted each spring.

Occasionally, we recalled the Beatrix Potter stories we had read to our young daughters about Peter Rabbit – and the awful Mr. McGregor, whose vegetable garden Peter raided.

Back then, we sided with cute little Peter, of course. Who was to know that one day we would feel such empathy for Mr. and Mrs. McGregor?

Unlike the McGregors, we hadn't yet made rabbit pie; that would be going a bit too far. But, depending on how much damage had been done to the vegetable garden on any particular day, we sighed heavily, swore lightly, or shouted threats. Didn't do a thing to stop the rabbits, of course. But for a very brief moment, we felt better.

Chapter Five

A Visit with Dr. Helen

The book launch was only four days away.

"All you have to do is show up," Reverend Claire had said a few weeks earlier. "We're doing everything else. Can you handle a few short readings from your book?"

Our priest was so enthusiastic, I couldn't imagine telling her no.

"And make a few remarks?" she added.

I laughed. "And make a few remarks? You're pushing your luck, Reverend Claire!"

She laughed back. I loved her laugh.

So I obediently agreed to read from my newly released book on May 18, at St. Thomas' Anglican in Brooklin, near the Blue House where we had lived.

~

It was to be a breakfast event, organized by Reverend Claire and a small group of church members responsible for the monthly Women's Reflection Breakfasts.

"My life is about to change," I told myself, not quite believing it. "I will become an author."

After years of failure, years without a professional identity, I was going to be something. This new identity would be launched in a place where I felt safe: my church community. In one fell swoop, I would go from being the parishioner who limped and wobbled and sometimes stuttered to being the author with the clearly written, coherent book.

I pictured how it would all unfold. It would be my first time doing this, so I would choose the excerpts beforehand and practice reading them. At the launch, I would read aloud from my book. Then I would sign copies for audience members.

Thinking about the proceedings was both exhilarating and terrifying. I did my best to focus on exhilaration. I hoped the parishioners would enjoy the reading. I hoped they would buy books. I planned to donate a chunk of the proceeds to the church.

Most of all, I hoped my husband and children would be happy. No matter how much they protested, I often felt ashamed of the person I had become. I wanted them to be proud of me.

But first, there was a crucial appointment with Dr. Helen.

~

I visited Dr. Helen at least twice each year: once in the fall and once in the spring. Between those appointments were all the other tests and visits to doctors and therapists who were monitoring my various treatments.

I sat with Dr. Helen in one of the hospital rooms I'd come to know so well. The kind that doctors use for examinations. It was clean, white, sterile. But the warmth emanating from this doctor – the trauma and rehabilitation specialist who years earlier had commanded me to "write" – always helped to calm me.

She was, I told myself, the kind of woman I would like to be when I grew up.

Her hair was cut stylishly short, her clothing was high quality but understated. She exuded a calm authority, whether she was asking a question or giving an expert opinion. It all added up to confidence and power, the kind that didn't need to shout but simply was.

A soft voice sounded from a distant memory place: *you were that kind of woman, once.*

~

The doctor was waiting for me to speak.

We both knew I still had a long recovery ahead of me. But for the first time in what felt like forever, I had some progress to report.

"I've been exercising my left arm steadily," I said, cautiously. "Hurts like hell, but I'm finally seeing progress. I can lift it higher now."

In earlier years, I had made minimal headway with my arm and shoulder. Each of several serious attempts had ended in surrender when pain, depression, or persistently recurring nightmares knocked me off my feet. But this time, I had finally hung in.

"Good," she replied. She proceeded to examine me – neck, arm, back, leg, hip, and foot – asking many questions along the way.

She didn't have to tell me I was still having memory problems – I knew.

I was surprised by what she said next.

"You're not driving anymore, are you, Cynthia?" Her tone said it was a foregone conclusion that no one in my condition would even attempt such a thing.

"Rarely."

"You mean that you *do* drive sometimes? You go on the road?"

My stomach lurched. "Yes, but not in rush hour, bad weather, or on very busy roads. Or at night."

I was stuttering badly now, desperately trying to reassure her while fear hammered away at my heart. "I drive to the library ... or my family doctor ... or therapist, and sometimes ... sometimes, I have to drive myself to the rehabilitation hospital. But that's about it. My husband drives the rest of the time."

"Oh."

"Why do you ask? No one told me to stop driving."

Dr. Helen was silent for just a moment too long.

"I've worked so hard to get more mobility in my neck and left shoulder!" I almost shouted, my words becoming even more fractured. "So ... so no one would tell me to stop driving. I need to drive!"

Dr. Helen looked away. "We'll have to send you for a driver's exam."

My stomach lurched again.

"And for more brain scans."

Aha. The brain stuff. The stuff that made me really anxious.

~

If there's a gun in the first part of a story, the writer must make sure it is fired before the end of the story, said Anton Chekhov. You can't just leave something like a gun hanging around. Something has to happen.

I had subconsciously been waiting for the gun to go off for some time now.

Never mind the gun. Since confirmation of the things that scared me most – post-traumatic stress disorder and a head injury – a gallows had been looming over me. Or, even worse, a room in an Alzheimer's ward.

People who have two hard blows to the head are at greater risk of developing some form of dementia. I'd had one from the accident and one from a subsequent fall down the stairs when my injured leg collapsed.

"The brain scans are to monitor the head injury," the doctor was telling me. "To see if it has progressed."

I heard her from a frightened distance.

"I'll need to see you more often, too." Her words conveyed a gentle sympathy alongside some other thing.

I looked away from her sympathy and that other thing, not wanting to see it, not wanting to feel it.

~

Anxieties over my head injury manifested themselves in a single fear now: losing my driver's licence.

It's not that I drove a lot. I didn't. But having the licence meant that I could. In a life so seriously compromised, that *could* represented a cherished bit of independence.

You might think that driving a car would be difficult for me, and for the first year or so, it was. But there was something much worse: being driven by someone else. A short drive in a taxi was torture. Even my husband, who had taken me to many appointments over the years since the accident, could barely handle being in the same car with me.

I had learned to muffle the screams, to close my eyes, to look away from the road, but the sight or sound of another car too near to ours still frightened me.

Without my licence, I now asked myself, how would I get to the library?

Strange what one thinks about at such times.

Then the concern that should have come first: How will I get to the hospital? After all, if my head injury did worsen, I would likely need more such visits.

And finally, the now-familiar dread: Would I become housebound all over again? Just when I was feeling so hopeful?

I said a prayer for strength and acceptance. But acceptance was nowhere in sight. Instead, I tasted the old feelings bubbling up: isolation, loss of independence, helplessness.

~

Back at home, Hamlin held his arms open wide, and I walked unsteadily into them. There was comfort in the warmth of his chest, the certainty of his strength. We stood like this for a long moment.

"I know what you should do," he finally said, in the tone of one who has just made a big discovery.

"Hmm-hmmm?" I said, my voice muffled against his chest.

"Just stop going to doctors. Stop. They're not good for you."

I pulled back from his arms and looked him in the face. "Tell me you're joking."

I knew every centimetre of this beloved man's face, every look it was capable of expressing. A long marriage will do that to observant partners. But even so, there were moments when I couldn't be sure. He would say something, and I would take it seriously, until he smiled and I realized I had missed the twinkle in his eyes.

I searched his face now. His brown eyes looked back at me. Steady. Loving. Twinkle-less.

"I'm not joking. You leave home full of hope – every time – and you come home demolished. *Every time.* What good are these visits doing you? Maybe it's time you stopped seeing doctors."

I burst out laughing. It was like the sun coming out in the middle of a rainstorm, because tears were still rolling down my cheeks.

"Don't know why I'm laughing," I said, sniffling. "This isn't funny. There are days I think I should have my head examined."

And days when a person says exactly the wrong thing. We both burst out laughing this time.

"We could probably write a book about all the crazy, screwy things I've come out with since this car accident happened," I said.

But I was wondering about what he said. Could I really quit doctors – cold turkey? Would it improve anything?

Chapter Six

My Church Throws a Party

And then it was May 17, only one day before the book launch.

The prospect of it almost banished worries of worsening brain damage and losing my licence. Silly fears popped into my head instead.

"Oh, no!" I said to Hamlin. "People at our church are going to read the part where you and I stripped off our clothes and ran naked through the backyard at the Blue House!"

After years of worrying about me, Hamlin had deciphered when an issue demanded serious scrutiny and when not. This time, he barely looked up from the book he was reading, raised his eyebrows, and said, casually, "So? Are you telling me they've never been naked?"

For a brief instant, I imagined a group of our church members standing in the buff.

"Perish the thought!" I said, smiling.

Indeed, there were more important things to worry about.

I feared I would stutter or cry while reading. Though I had written out every word I planned to say, I feared I would lose my place, or, worse, that the things I had tried so hard to hide would reveal themselves.

If I was lucky I'd be reduced to tears. If I wasn't, I would feel choked, would struggle to breathe, would even forget where I was. And when I recovered, my whole body would feel beaten up and I would be able to manage only a bad stutter. Then would come the crushing shame.

I was also sure some members of the audience would think less of me when I read the part about my shaky faith. After all, their faith in God seemed so strong.

"Telling the truth may get you into heaven, but it can cause a lot of problems here on earth," I fretted to Hamlin again. If he heard me, he didn't show it.

But I was determined to read that part of my book at the launch. This was my church, and these were my people. I wanted them to hear my admission from my own lips before they read it.

"Yes," I planned to say, "my faith gets very wobbly. And though I always pray, there are still a few times when I can hardly believe that God is listening."

After all, if you can't confess your failings in church, where can you do it?

~

St. Thomas' Anglican in the village of Brooklin, northeast of Toronto, used to be known as the little white church on the corner. It started life in 1869 as a one-room building, made in a style called Carpenter Gothic. The exterior is board and batten, with tall, narrow, arched windows.

But the village grew. By 2003, the main service – the one at 10:30 a.m. – was bursting at the seams. In 2009, an impressive new church was built right beside the old one, making it all one grand building under one very big roof.

The new sanctuary could accommodate more than three hundred people. Huge wooden buttresses followed the line of the walls and the sloped ceiling, a modern take on the stone arches of ancient Christian cathedrals.

Hamlin and I continued to attend the 8:30 a.m. service in the old sanctuary, now known as "the chapel." It had not changed, except to become a little more timeworn. With pastel-coloured stained glass windows filtering the light, the space remained intimate. Average Sunday morning attendance? Thirty souls. This qualified as major growth: when I started attending this service in the late 1990s, the average was nine.

~

Between the new church and the old chapel lies the church hall, which, in good Anglican fashion, we call the parish hall. Everything from coffee hour to vestry (our annual church business meeting) to suppers and receptions – for christenings, weddings, anniversaries, and funerals – is held here.

The event organizers had pulled out all the stops. Every table in the parish hall sported a nice tablecloth and a vase of flowers. Almost every table was full, and men were in attendance, as well. I knew almost everyone there, and they knew me.

Years earlier, before my accident, I had been church warden. In that role, I had played a leading role in buying the land next door so we could build our large new church and extend this hall. Just a few years later, Hamlin co-chaired the committee that raised funds to build the new church. Most people here today had donated to that cause.

I walked over to the tables, Hamlin and daughter Lauren by my side, stopping to thank everyone for showing up on the Saturday morning of a long weekend.

"I know why you're here," I said to a few of the men. "Your wives forced you to attend!"

"No, no! We are really looking forward to it!" they replied.

One after another, parishioners stood to hug me, telling me they were happy for me, patting me gently on the back. Some pointed out that St. Thomas' had never held a book launch before.

This should be a joyous event, I told myself. If I can get through it.

By now our older daughter, Nikisha, was living in Seattle with her husband, Tim. Tim had put in his order even before the book was available for sale and had joyfully called to announce that he was the first person in the United States to buy the book.

I wished they could have attended but knew they couldn't. They had arrived in their new city only two months earlier, and Tim had already started his new job.

Hamlin and Lauren sat nearby as I read, beaming love and pride. So did my sister Pat and brother-in-law Keith. A few close friends had driven all the way from Toronto, as did my publisher and his wife.

Wherever I looked, friendly faces looked back at me. Jane at one table, Muriel and Michael at another, Joanne and Tony at still another, all beaming encouragement. Georgeina, Judy, Doreen. Bryan, Bob and Peter. Dorothy, Dianne, Betty and Babs. Don and June. Lucia and Kingsley, both long-time friends. Karen, Desrine. Dozens of others.

A wave of support rolled toward my shore.

Yes, I was frightened. Yes, there were long moments where I could not speak. And of course, I cried. There were also moments when I had to look away from the audience, because many of them were crying.

In the end, the event was strengthening, with much laughter and love, many smiles and nods, and dozens of books sold.

"I hope I didn't let you down," I told Rev. Claire when

we had a quiet moment together. "Telling churchgoers my faith is weak is a risky thing."

"You didn't let me down one bit," she said in that assured tone of voice I had grown to treasure. "If anyone tells you they've never had moments of doubt – even whole periods of doubt – don't believe it. We're all human, you know."

"Yes," I said. "I know."

Chapter Seven

An Oath of Cowardice

Faith is one thing. But courage? That is a whole different matter.

I sat at the harvest table in the kitchen, a cup of coffee in front of me, telling myself that cowardice wasn't such a bad thing, after all; in fact, sometimes it was the only option. This was one of those times.

I was lying to myself, hoping my self would believe it.

I leaned back in my chair, sipped the coffee, and looked at the room around me. The cupboards were the same ones the previous owners had installed. Sturdy, made from oak, they had been varnished by time into a mellow brown.

The fridge and oven were several years old; the stovetop was as old as the cabinets but still worked perfectly.

Between the cooking part of the room and the sitting part was an antique hutch. We had separated its two vertical sections and placed them on the floor, back to back, making it easier for me to reach their contents. One section held deep shelves and drawers; the other, fronted by mullioned glass doors, held three shelves.

And then there was the harvest table, which, across

more than a hundred years, had acquired a patina similar to the shade of the oak cupboards.

Not modern, this room and its contents, but comfortable. And the perfect place for someone determined to stay home and hide from doctors. Which is why, when the phone rang, I decided to ignore it. I sipped some more coffee. Slowly.

～

Restlessly, I reached for the newspaper Hamlin had left at one end of the table, but put it back down. What would I do if they took away my licence? I wondered. Our home wasn't on the bus route. The four places I visited regularly required a car. The hospital was one, the library another. Hamlin always drove me to the other two: our church and Costco.

All of these places provided me with sustenance.

The hospital helped mend my body. Or tried to. Caring doctors and physical therapy helped me deal with the pain.

Church mended my soul. Or tried to. It was a place of love and support, a place where my wobbly faith got shored up, at least while I was there.

Costco provided me with a multi-use facility. While Hamlin used one shopping cart to pick up groceries and home supplies, I gently pushed another up and down the wide aisles for exercise. I'm pretty sure the people who designed these aisles didn't know they would be used for this purpose. But, for me, a shopping cart was a less humiliating version of a walker and easier than my cane, which I shoved into the cart soon after entering the store.

And then there was the library. The library helped me to escape the confines of my reduced life. Reading inspired me, informed me, and allowed me to break out of my narrow world, at least for a time.

In earlier years, I could have made the long walk to the library and would have done so gladly. Now, with pain from my back to my foot, and a tendency to fall, I would be foolish to try.

I still fantasized about long walks. The lovely, long ones I used to take with Hamlin and our pet dog Kinu in the woods near our home. Such simple, carefree times.

What will I do? I wondered.

The one thing you will not do, I lectured myself, is curl up into a ball of depression.

～

"My best advice is to find somewhere warm to live between November and April," my specialist, Dr. Helen, had said two years earlier.

For two years, I had gone to pain management sessions at Toronto's best-known rehabilitation hospital – Toronto Rehab – sent there by Dr. Helen. The therapists there taught me a lot about how to manage pain without using drugs, but the winter months were particularly difficult. In desperation, I asked the doctor for further help – something other than drugs that could help me lessen the pain.

Her recommendation of decamping for the south for five months took me by surprise. It had been such a long time since Hamlin and I had even taken a short vacation. Live somewhere else for several months? As if, I muttered to myself. As if we could afford such a luxury.

But late at night, when everyone else was asleep, I wished we could travel somewhere warm the next winter. The milder temperatures would help, I knew. It's what I would do if I won the lottery, I thought, forgetting that I rarely played the lottery.

～

"Maybe you can get a licence to drive in a different country," said a little voice in the back of my head as I sat in my kitchen hideout.

"And maybe I'll be in such bad shape that not being able to drive will be the least of my worries," I answered.

The phone rang again. Again, I waited for it to stop.

I had taken an oath of cowardice, and I was sticking to it.

Chapter Eight

A Call from Aunt Rose

Sunshine poured through the windows, bathing our wooden floors and furniture in the mellow northwestern light of late afternoon. The old harvest table, made of four long, dark, burnished planks of hard maple, glowed.

It was Sunday afternoon. I stood and stared absently at the effect of the sun's rays then back at the cookbook on the counter in front of me.

Why on earth had I insisted on making Sunday dinner? In our home it was expected to be a cut above normal fare.

My thoughts flitted from one thing to another.

Nikisha and Tim always called on a Sunday afternoon. I glanced at the clock. It wasn't time yet.

Reader reaction to the book came to mind, and I said a prayer of thanks for its early success.

The pain in my back, leg, and foot had become worse. I had surrendered and taken a painkiller, but it didn't seem to be working.

The thought of losing my licence floated in and out of my mind, too, but I banished it.

The phone rang. I figured it was safe to answer; it was a Sunday, after all. Recognizing the number on the display,

I grabbed the receiver then a pen and whatever was handy to write on.

"Dahling?" the caller said in that lovely Jamaican lilt of female relatives in the older generations of our family.

"Hello, my dear Aunt Rose," I said.

"How are you?"

"I'm fine, Aunt Rose. Especially now that I'm talking to you. How are you?"

"I'm fine, too, Dahling."

Her voice, coming to me from her home in New Jersey, took on a slightly aggrieved tone. "But why don't you call? I don't hear from you at all."

Before I could defend myself, she continued: "At my age, I shouldn't have to be the one calling all you young people all the time. You should be calling me."

"That's so true, Aunt Rose. You're absolutely right."

"If I'm so right, why don't you call more often?"

"Aunt Rose, I do call. I left a message on your phone just last week. Did you not get it?"

She was not backing down. "No," she said firmly. "I didn't get any message."

Truth is, even at 107 years old, her memory was better than mine. I bet she didn't have notebooks in every room to remind her of those she talked to an hour ago and what they said. Plus, I had a problem placing things in their proper time. It could have been a month ago that I called her.

I tried a different tack. "So how are you, my darling aunt?"

Her voice softened. She recited a short list of ailments. Followed, as usual, by: "But I'm still here, giving God thanks."

"I sent you a copy of the book, as promised."

"Thank you, Dahling."

"I couldn't have written it without you, Aunt Rose. So I'm the one who should be saying thanks. Thank you, my dear aunt."

Aunt Rose's sharp memory had filled some of the gaps in our family history, and she had verified several of the tales in the book.

I always made sure I could take notes when she called: she always shared something worth jotting down. That, plus the fact that my own memory was so bad, I knew she would trip me up with her remarkable ability to recall items we had discussed earlier.

You know you're in bad shape when your 107-year-old aunt has to remind you about things that only recently took place.

~

Aunt Rose never forgot to call. It was as if she was determined to keep my spirits buoyed, help me rebuild my faith in myself, keep me connected to the faith and strength of my forebears.

But she also loved to tease me.

Always, she asked about my siblings and children. And, always, the conversation eventually turned to her favourite person in my house.

"How's my boyfriend?" she would ask, giggling like a schoolgirl.

"He's fine. Always sends his love to you."

"Well, you tell him I send my love to him, too!"

My great-aunt claimed to have a crush on Hamlin, and she never let me forget it.

"I'm glad you're twice my husband's age and living in another country," I always told her. "I couldn't stand the competition!"

She had called one day several months earlier while Hamlin, the gourmet chef in our family, was cooking dinner. She had insisted I relay her love to him while she was on the phone.

"Your favourite girlfriend sends her love," I yelled across the kitchen.

"Tell her I wish she were here," he called back, laughing.

Aunt Rose giggled happily. "You tell my boyfriend if I was just a little bit younger, I'd give you a run for your money!"

"Oh, yeah?" Hamlin replied when I told him. "Ask her what's 'a little bit younger.'"

Aunt Rose's laugh was louder now. "Well, maybe just twenty years or so. Not much."

～

"Let me know when you get the book," I said to her now. "I hope you like it, but I also know you'll tell me the truth, like it or not."

We laughed some more, said a loving goodbye, and I returned to the puzzle of dinner.

Chapter Nine

Tuesdays with Sarah

Strange as it may seem, I was avoiding my doctors, but not my therapists. Or not so strange: no therapist had ever threatened to have my driver's licence taken away.

Therapy helped me cope with my injuries, both physical and psychological.

Lynette, who once told me I was the angriest patient she'd met in her decades of pain management work at the rehabilitation hospital, had retired. The pool sessions were now being led by a physiotherapist named John. I teased him that Lynette had softened me up for him, that he was getting a far kinder, gentler outpatient now.

It didn't matter how much pain I was in when I got there; I almost always left with a smile on my face. The hot water and exercises always worked their magic.

"John," I asked one day after the session ended, "could I just live here in this pool?"

He smiled. "A lot of people wish the same thing. It does relieve the pain, doesn't it?"

"Yes, at least for a while. It's nowhere as painful as on dry land. And I feel accomplished, because I've worked hard."

I was also still seeing therapist Sarah for help against

the thing I could barely bring myself to think about – post-traumatic stress disorder – and its close ally, depression.

I dreaded these sessions. Not because of Sarah, but because talking about the accident, the terrors that plagued my nights, or the flashbacks that hounded my days was like opening a door wide and inviting the PTSD monster to come in and beat me up.

For nearly a year, I refused to discuss these things with Sarah, and she wisely refrained from pushing me. Yet I knew talking about them with her was the only way she could help me find a way out of the darkness.

As she and I worked our way forward over long months, every step took me into enemy territory. Each session triggered the anxiety attacks. Each discussion brought scalding tears, blinding headaches, and tightness in my throat, chest, and entire body.

I had no idea how long each episode lasted, or exactly what happened, but it always felt as if I had entered a very dark and dangerous forest. Time stopped in that forest. Then a voice would call out, as if from a great distance: "Cynthia, open your eyes. Open your eyes, Cynthia. You're here with me. You're safe."

When I finally opened my eyes, I was always surprised to find myself sitting across from Sarah.

Sarah was younger than I, perhaps in her late thirties. She was petite, blonde, and pleasant. But most important to me, she never pushed beyond where I was willing to go.

At the end of every session, she encouraged me to ask questions or share observations.

"There is something I only noticed recently," I told her. "When the anxiety attacks are over, my whole body feels beaten up. It can stay that way for hours or even days."

Sarah listened intently.

"I think I finally know why," I said.

"Why?"

"While the episode is going on, my body tightens up as if to protect me. It's like my body is battling with itself."

Sarah knew I still couldn't bring myself to read much about PTSD. I was practicing the fine art of avoidance. Some of what she shared – findings of studies about PTSD – was information I already knew from experience, but some confirmed suspicions that I had never voiced.

Bit by bit, when she felt I was ready to hear, she explained how PTSD works. How traumatic experiences are held in the body for years, and perhaps even a lifetime.

I shuddered at that thought. Who wants an alien monster residing in one's body forever?

At the end of every session, Sarah reminded me of the progress she had seen me make over our time together. It was part of the pact we had made at the beginning of my therapy: that she would reinforce any positive development.

"You recently used the full term, 'post-traumatic stress disorder,'" she noted one day. "For at least a year you never called it by name. You always called it 'The Thing.'"

Yes, I had. And still did, most of the time. "To name it was to admit it existed," I confessed. "I was too frightened to do even that."

Another day, after a full-blown anxiety attack in her office, after the deep breathing and the calming down, she turned to an image on a sheet of paper. Together, we had created a picture of a mountain that represented my recovery. It looked daunting at first, but then Sarah asked me to identify some of the strengths and tools I could call on.

Family was the first word we placed at the base of the mountain. Friends, we wrote next. Then, my faith in God. And my church. Then we wrote down doctors and therapists. Then my writing.

Sarah noted that, despite the trauma and despair of the

last several years, I hadn't lost my core values. I still knew when something felt right or wrong, even if I couldn't always explain why.

So we added core values.

"And your type A personality. We should add that, too."

I frowned at this. I frequently blamed my perfectionist personality for bringing The Thing to life.

"I'm willing to bet type A people suffer more from this Thing than other people do," I told her. "We want to control everything. And then, when we find ourselves unable to control a little thing like a car accident, we go nuts."

"But it's also your type A personality that makes you so determined to recover," she said. "Even your approach to therapy is purposeful. You want to set goals and find out whether you are making progress. Those are good traits."

As Sarah detected progress, more items were added to the picture of the mountain.

I was becoming a mountaineer.

~

When the manuscript of my memoir was being edited, I needed to rewrite some of what I called "the difficult bits." These were the final chapters of the book, the ones that covered the years after the accident.

I had already transferred much of what I had written to my computer from journals and notebooks, and asked therapist Sarah, my family, and close friends to help me fact check it. All this had taken a toll, sending me back to bed – a trembling, weeping mess – for weeks.

Now, despite all the help, and that of Don, my editor and publisher, I didn't think I could survive what he was asking me to do.

"Revisiting those final chapters will just finish me off," I fretted to Hamlin.

"No, it won't," he'd say. "Look how far you've come. The journey is almost over."

But of course it wasn't.

~

I was in a mighty mess when I arrived for my next session with Sarah. She had agreed to see me on an emergency basis. She met me at the gate beside her office building and led me down the narrow gravel path to the garden.

The summer before, knowing how much I hated stairs, and how much I liked gardens, Sarah had started holding our sessions in a garden studio. It was a one-room building behind the therapy centre in downtown Toronto where she had her office.

The walls were cedar-clad. The windows were large. A small front porch provided a transition between the garden and the studio. Perennials grew in the garden in front. Tree branches hung over the building, and sometimes I watched them swaying through the skylight.

It was a welcoming space inside, with two chairs facing each other, a small table, and a large box of Kleenex. Even in winter, we continued our sessions there, warmed by a space heater and the room's insulated walls.

I sank gratefully into a chair, determined to ignore the throbbing pain in my back and leg. Sarah started the session with a short meditation, as she always did. But as soon as it ended, I blurted, "I can't continue with this book!"

"What happened? Can you talk about it?"

"I have to revisit the final chapters, and I can't do it. I've been trembling and stuttering, and the pain is worse, and I haven't slept in days, and I'm crying all the time, and ..."

"It's been a very tough time. I'm not surprised it's affecting you in this way. Anyone would be rattled by it, Cynthia."

"But if I can't even read that stuff without having a breakdown, Sarah, how am I ever going to talk about the book? Oh, my God ... people are going to expect me to talk about it after the book's published. Oh, God!"

I was shaking, trembling, stuttering, crying. A vicious ache blazed across my head. My throat tightened up, burning. I could almost see the monster approaching. I started to close my eyes.

"Don't close your eyes, Cynthia. Open your eyes. Open your eyes ... Breathe ..."

After what felt like forever, I opened my eyes. We started the breathing exercises. It calmed me. For a few minutes.

"I'm cancelling the book," I said. "I'm not ready for any of this. I'm cancelling it. Maybe a few years from now ..."

~

Later that day, I asked Don to join Hamlin and me on a conference call. Sarah and Hamlin both felt I had to talk to him.

"I've been thinking of cancelling the book," I said, citing the same reasons I had given Sarah.

Hamlin reached out and hugged me, rubbing my shoulder gently.

Don, who undoubtedly had dealt with temperamental authors before, spoke in a calm and measured voice. "We don't have to decide right now, Cynthia. We'll delay publication till you're ready."

That was what Sarah had suggested, but I had signed a contract and hadn't thought Don would agree. Now he was suggesting it himself.

I had been to the precipice and come back. The book would be published, but only when I was ready. I allowed myself to feel relief.

But there was still much work to do.

~

Sarah suggested using part of our weekly sessions to prepare me for talking about the book after it was published.

Every week, we worked on what I jokingly called my author's toolkit: the skills that would help me cope.

What to do if I started to stutter.

What to do if I forgot what I was saying, or burst into tears.

What to do if I suddenly felt that I was choking or blacking out.

She offered a few more suggestions. Setting limits was one.

"You should never feel you have to discuss something that makes you uncomfortable. If you have to do a book reading, or be interviewed, set limits on which sections of the book you'll read and the topics you'll discuss."

It felt very strange. A former interviewer myself, I would have considered this very odd behaviour coming from an author. But the alternative – refusing to talk at all about the book – seemed crazy. So this tactic went into the toolkit along with the others.

Another suggestion was to write point-form notes on paper. These were meant to guide my remarks but also could be read.

"And always, always make sure your husband or a relative or close friend is with you. Someone who will recognize when you're heading into trouble. Someone who can ground you and remind you that you're safe."

The fourth and perhaps most important recommendation was to pace my activities very carefully. I was to take on only as much as I could confidently manage; I was to plan time for physiotherapy, daily exercises, and – just as important – for rest.

~

When *A Good Home* had finally been published, I handed Sarah a signed copy of the book, gave her a warm hug for the first time, and promised I would follow her advice. We had been through such a long and challenging journey together, and though we had made progress, we both knew that the journey wasn't over.

Chapter Ten

My Family

By late June, sales of *A Good Home* were taking off. The book made it onto the bestseller lists of two categories on Amazon: biographies in general, and memoirs by women.

Reader reviews started popping up on various book sites, all highly positive. And every day, I got emails from people who had just finished reading the book.

One woman said, "I just didn't want it to end. So when I got to the end, I went back to the beginning and read it for a second time."

My family and I basked in the praise. Hamlin and I called Nikisha and Tim in Seattle one evening.

"Can you believe that?" I asked them, doing my lopsided version of a jig where I stood in the kitchen. "They said they didn't want the story to end! They reread the last several chapters. They reread the whole book. And they wanted to know when book two will be ready!"

I was thrilled.

Then taken aback.

The jigging stopped.

Book two? I couldn't believe it. "Do they have any idea

what it took out of me to write book number one?" I asked Hamlin.

"Why not another one?" he asked, with a big smile.

"Why not? All told, it took more than thirty years to write book number one! And then writing the last chapters nearly killed me!"

But before I could even think of a sequel, I had some tasks to take care of. I had thanked my immediate family, but there were others in my family – and in my larger "village" – who had helped bring me this far.

~

I gave each of my four siblings a copy of the book, inscribed with a heartfelt message of thanks. My sisters Yvonne and Jackie and brother Michael – each made the memoir stronger, whether with a vivid memory of a childhood event, a saying by our mother or grandmother, or a bit of insight that helped me understand our family better.

And then there was Pat, my elder sister by a few years.

Asking Pat to read the manuscript was like turning a tap on at full gush. She remembered a dozen stories from our childhood that "should be included in the book."

"Stop!" I finally said. "It's too late! The book has gone to press."

Even after it was published and she held her own copy, she kept remembering stories in such detail and with such hilarity that I told her I didn't know why I was the author when she clearly was the storyteller in the family.

~

The stories continued to come, jointly told by Pat and me at family dinners. They lifted my spirits and helped daughter Lauren learn more about our childhood in the Jamaican countryside.

"And what about the time when we decided to run

away?" Pat said at a Sunday dinner that spring. She put her fork down and sent me a stern look. "How could you have forgotten to put that one in the book?"

"Right. Yet another time I followed you straight into trouble."

"Well ... I was a bad big sister." She wore her delinquency like a badge of honour. "And you were such a faithful follower. You followed me everywhere. But you had a lot of fun, didn't you?"

"Not always. Not the time we crouched under that house cellar for hours in the dark, waiting to run away ..."

～

In the great migration of Jamaican men to England in the 1950s and early 1960s, our father went to work in London. Mama and the five of us children moved in with our grandmother in her large home in a nearby village.

Grandmother was a very proper woman, respected far and wide as a nurse, church deaconess, and community leader. To her, we children were like wild animals. We roamed fields, scampered up tall trees, climbed through or over wire fences, and stole the neighbours' fruit.

One neighbour was a retired policeman everyone called Corporal. One day, after we had sneaked through his fence and stolen yet more tangerines and star apples, he threatened to shoot us.

Grandmother was ashamed. First, we had violated her orderly home, and then her relations with the neighbours. But worse was to come.

One day, after raiding Corporal's fruit trees, we came home very late for supper, our dresses torn, our feet, hands, and faces streaked with dirt. We had a feeling that Corporal had complained again to Grandmother.

Just days before, Grandmother had told our mother

that we children were making her life "a living hell." From all those Sundays in church, Pat and I knew hell was A Very Bad Place, and we felt ashamed of ourselves. But our shame didn't last.

Now, as we hid behind a breadfruit tree near the house, we dreaded the punishment that awaited us.

"We should run away," Pat said. Out of the blue, just like that, she said it.

I searched her face. She was serious.

"Let's hide in the cellar till they go to bed," she said. "Then we'll run away."

It made sense at the time.

We heard our mother calling for us, but the longer we stayed in the cellar, the more afraid we were to reply. Crouching in the darkness on the dirt floor, we waited for her to stop calling.

But when she stopped, that was even scarier. No rooster crowed. No hens clucked. No dogs barked. The birds had long stopped their singing, the crickets their chirping.

We had no idea how long we had been in the cellar. Then we heard something scratching on wood, way too close.

"Pat," I whispered.

"What?"

"Where are we going to run away to?"

Even in the darkness, I could tell she was surprised.

"I don't know."

This was shocking. Pat always had a plan.

"Well, we better go inside and take the punishment," she said.

Ever defiant, she made a pledge with me: if we were punished, we'd return to stealing the neighbours' fruit. If we weren't, we'd stop.

We crept out, knees hurting, and shook the dirt from our skirts. Our stomachs growled with hunger.

The back door was unlocked. We went in and found Mama at her sewing machine.

She smiled at us. "You finally decided to come in?"

Grandmother stood beside her, stern, but, surprisingly, said nothing.

We washed up, ate our supper, and went to bed.

Pat and I figured it out much later: Mama must have divined where we were hiding and convinced Grandmother that hours in a dark cellar was punishment enough.

~

My siblings, our Aunt Rose in New Jersey, our uncles in England, and our cousin Norma – also in England – were part of a support network that never failed me through those anguished years after the accident.

My siblings called often, checking on me, encouraging me, and reminding me of our mother's uplifting sayings.

One day, when younger sister Jackie called from New York and asked how I was feeling, I wondered aloud how long I could continue to live in such pain and misery.

She was quick to reply. "Remember the man with the banana peel?"

"Oh, God," I groaned. "How could anyone in our family ever forget that story?" Mama had told it to us many times.

"I think you need to remember it right now," Jackie said. Without waiting for my answer, she began to recite it.

"There was once a man who lost everything he owned, and everyone he loved. All he had left were the clothes on his back and one ripe banana. He decided he may as well eat that last bit of food and then go drown himself. So he walked along the road to the river, ate the banana, and threw the peel on the ground. Some while later, he looked behind him. There was a man in ragged clothes eating the banana peel he had dropped on the ground.

"As the man watched this stranger eat that banana peel, he realized that, no matter how bad things were for him, someone was a lot worse off. He at least had had a banana to eat. In that moment, he decided that he would not kill himself after all."

It was Jackie who spoke but Mama's voice that I heard. It bore all the love, along with the firmness and moral authority that I remembered so well.

My siblings knew that some days the deep waters threatened to pull me under. They were determined to keep me afloat.

Chapter Eleven

Our Neighbours

Down the street from the farmhouse, neighbours Paddy and Jacqui were in renovation hell.

Workmen had been overhauling their upstairs bathroom, and the work should have been completed by now. But the beautiful granite counter – the finishing touch – arrived unpolished.

"They have to come back to polish it," Paddy told me on the phone. "Lord knows how much longer we're going to have to wait till we can use our sink again."

Paddy's lilting Jamaican accent had taken on a tone of disgust for such sloppiness.

"We must have a bathroom party when it's finally complete," I said, trying to cheer him up. "How many people can you fit in the bathroom at a time?"

Months earlier, I had phoned Paddy and Jacqui, read them the sections of my manuscript in which they were mentioned, and received their approval.

But when they came over for their copy of the book, they seemed surprised. "Thank you!" Paddy said, examining both front and back covers. "This is very nice. And it's the first time anyone ever put my name in a book!"

Back at home, Paddy read the chapter where he and his

wife were mentioned and phoned to tell me I got Jacqui's name wrong.

"There's no 'e' on the end of 'Jacqui.'"

"Yikes!" I said. "A typo. I hate typos."

Paddy laughed. "Don't worry, you can call us anything you want. After everything you've been through, we're just glad you got the book published And I tell you, Cynthia, it's a really good book. Thanks again."

~

Just a few doors away, Diane, who kindly supplied us with raspberry jam – and sometimes maple syrup from the farms of her relatives in Quebec – had been trying to revive my French-language skills. Although fully bilingual, she spoke to me mostly in French.

These days, I no longer spoke French, Spanish, or Italian fluently. Heck, on some days I had a tough time speaking my first language, English. Diane, however, always told me my French was still there. "You haven't lost it."

And so she continued speaking in French, slowing down just a little to allow me to catch up. Sometimes I got lost. Sometimes I understood her perfectly but couldn't find the words to reply. Once in a while I answered her in French without even realizing it.

"See? It's there. I told you!" she would say, in French. "That is a very good sign."

Diane was a gracious and kind woman who always tried to see the best in everything. But it had been a tough year for her. Her husband, Art, had died after being ill for several months. She missed him terribly and was trying to keep herself busy.

"Come for tea," she invited me one day as I passed her house.

"Great! What day?"

"Well …" she said, "I have exercise class on Tuesday and Thursday mornings, then I have to go to …"

She finally squeezed me in on Tuesday afternoon. I decided to hand her the book then.

～

Next door, Matthew and Susie had returned home from yet another cruise. In recent years, they had travelled to Russia, Italy, and several other countries. Each time, before leaving, Matthew called and asked us to keep an eye on their house. He knew, without asking, that, if it was summer, Hamlin would also mow the lawn if it got too tall, or, if it was winter, clear the snow.

Matthew kept us supplied with broad beans and Asian vegetables from his garden and occasionally shared remedies for various ailments.

"Oh!" was all he said now, staring at the book I handed him as we stood in his front garden.

"Oh!" he said even more loudly when I showed him the reference to his wife and him. He seemed a little dazed as he said, "You wrote this … Cynthia?"

But he also seemed proud of me.

And then, he thanked me repeatedly and rushed back into the house to show Susie the book.

～

"You wrote this?" Kikki asked, her dark eyes opened wide in surprise.

I was the neighbour who was rarely seen outside my home, the reclusive woman who might get teary and walk away if asked the simple question neighbours routinely ask one another: How are you?

"Yes," I said, "over many years. I only recently finished it. Your names are mentioned on page 291, you and George."

"Our names are mentioned?"

I opened the book and showed her.

"Our names are in a book?"

Kikki and George were finally grandparents, of twins. Their daughter had been married for several years.

"We prayed for grandchildren since the wedding day," Kikki told me.

Now the twins were nearly a year old, and when they visited, Kikki and George had their hands full. But they were also in grandparent heaven.

~

Vito and Loretta were also grandparents. Their daughter and her family had recently moved in with them while a house was being built for them nearby. Loretta, a diabetic, now cooked for herself and Vito, who loved traditional Italian fare, and their expanded household.

"How do you manage it all?" I once asked her.

"I manage." Her shoulders rose and fell back into place, indicating resignation or at least stoicism. But I saw something else in her face: Loretta was happy to have everyone under her roof.

Vito, who, in one of my darkest hours, had reminded me to count my blessings, was now pretending to be calm as he held my book in his strong hands. But I could tell he was excited. When I opened the book to the page where he is mentioned the first time, a smile stole over his face. He was speechless for a long moment. That was not like him at all.

"We are ordinary people," he said at last, looking up at me then back down at the page. "We never knew anyone would ever write about us in a book."

My throat tightened, and my eyes felt a bit misty. I wanted to say something like, "But you are not ordinary people." But I didn't get the words out. I just smiled and touched his arm.

~

No, my neighbours weren't just ordinary people. Not in our family's eyes.

They had helped me up when I fell on the sidewalk.

Helped our pet dog Kinu when he, too, fell on the sidewalk and I couldn't help him up by myself. Waited patiently with him, rubbing his head, murmuring to him, for the whole time it took me to limp home to get Hamlin.

In big ways and little ways, they helped.

Our neighbours included passionate gardeners, vintners, cooks, and curers and preservers of meats, jams, and sauces. We knew this well: we had been blessed with gifts from their kitchens and cellars.

Kikki had even offered to teach me how to cook a few Greek dishes, while Diane said she would show me how to cook French food, and Loretta, Italian food.

I had said, "Sure," "Why not?" and "You really think I can learn?" But, with all my daylight hours spent on my recovery or on completing the book, I had never taken them up on their offers.

I also knew something they didn't know: I was a sub-par cook who occasionally got lucky when a recipe turned out well. And, since the accident, even simple dishes could stump me.

~

Tuesday came and I stood at Diane's kitchen counter as she prepared tea and cookies.

Diane's delight at the book made me smile.

"Oh, Cynthia!" she said, turning the book this way and that then back to the front cover. "This is merveilleux!"

I hugged her.

We sipped our tea, munched our cookies, chatted, and I got an idea. I asked if she still wanted to show me how to cook one or two of her favourite dishes.

"But they must be simple!" I said. "I can't do complicated."

"Let's see," she said, raising her eyebrows as she considered my question. "Crêpes, peut-être? Très façile. And ... Quebec pea soup! J'aime ça. And it is simple, yes, Cynthia!"

I smiled as she hopscotched between the two languages.

"Let's see: when should we do this?" asked Diane, as she considered her commitments for the months ahead.

We settled on two times in the fall. I smiled at her, sure I'd be feeling stronger by then.

～

This is what I will do in the coming year if I'm stuck at home, unable to drive myself anywhere, I thought on the walk home. I will write. And I will ask the neighbours to teach me how to cook.

"I still want to show you how to make moussaka," Kikki had said when I visited her a few days earlier. "Come when you feel well enough."

She reflected on this and added, "... and when the twins aren't visiting."

I decided to take her up on her offer once the eggplants in her garden and mine were harvested.

Maybe this time I'll become the great cook I never was, I thought. But as I approached my side door, I was already back-pedalling.

Or at least a half-decent cook, I told myself. Then again, more and more studies were saying that cognitive skills could be improved by doing things you've always found difficult.

That was it, then. I would find out if the claims were

true. I would write. And I would find out if I could ever become a real cook. I was tired of being afraid.

Relishing my good mood, I knew where my next excursion would be.

Chapter Twelve

The Library

Books.

One of the greatest inventions of all time.

Long before I ever travelled on an airplane, I flew to foreign lands by reading books.

My family in Jamaica could not afford to travel abroad for vacations. And though our entire family loved language and books, it was all my parents could do to find enough money to buy textbooks for their five children.

So I sought out the old library at my high school, Manchester School, in Mandeville, the largest city in our parish.

It was a one-room affair, with the musty smell of all old libraries. Its shelves were stacked from floor to ceiling with ancient-looking hardcover books. Their covers were clothbound in the faded shades I had come to associate with very old books: blue, cream, burgundy, and a washed-out shade of green.

My heart nearly burst the first time I entered. I was in Aladdin's Cave, a mysterious place full of treasures. Better yet, it was all mine. A big new library had been built next to the school years before, and this one stood unused.

Never did I see another living soul in this place, though I sneaked in to it every chance I got. Breaks. Lunch. Spares. I missed the bus a few times because I lost track of time, which meant walking the nearly two miles home under a blazing sun.

The shelves were crammed with books in several languages. Some were written in old languages. Latin, Greek, old English, and Spanish, French, and German.

"May I take these ones home?" I would ask a teacher, showing her two or three books I had chosen.

"You seem to be the only one who reads those old books," she said, peering at me over her glasses. "Yes, you may borrow them any time you want. Just write down the titles and names of the authors on a piece of paper and leave it with me."

I was in heaven.

Much later, I would learn that some of these books were rare first editions, decades-old gifts from aristocratic patrons. Ours was the oldest secondary school in Jamaica, and Mandeville had long been the favoured second home of upper-class Britons.

I didn't know any of that at the time, nor would it have mattered. I already knew these books were priceless. They were, after all, books.

~

It is a truth universally acknowledged that a watched pot never boils. And that a woman in pursuit of a very popular library book must possess considerable patience.

Or so Jane Austen might have thought, if she had been right there beside me.

It was a weekday morning, nearly two years before my book was published, and I stood waiting in my local library to get my hands on P.D. James' *Death Comes to Pemberley*. Across the counter from me, the librarian, a blonde, sixtyish woman with a calm presence, was also waiting. She had just finished typing a few words on her computer.

P.D. James is famous for her murder mystery novels, and this one is in a similar genre. But as every Jane Austen fan knows, Pemberley is the home of Mr. Darcy and his new wife, the former Miss Elizabeth Bennet. Several of Austen's *Pride and Prejudice* characters show up in this James book, including Mr. Darcy's sweet younger sister Georgiana, and even the nasty Mr. Wickham and his foolish wife, Lydia, Elizabeth's younger sister.

Word on the street was that James had nailed Austen's distinctive writing style. As a result of all the recent media coverage, James and Austen fans – and even some who were neither – were eagerly anticipating this novel.

So there I was, waiting for the librarian and her computer to perform their perambulations and give me the good news – that the book was hiding somewhere in the library or would be available soon.

"Done!" she said pleasantly.

"You've got it?"

"Oh, no ..." She smiled at my hopeful face. "I meant to say I've added you to the waiting list for it."

"How long will I have to wait?" I guessed it would take a week or two for the book to be sent from another library branch.

"Well, let's see ..." She looked at her computer screen again. "1341."

"Pardon?"

"You're number 1341."

"What does that mean?"

"That's your place on the waiting list."

"1341? That can't be right. Can you please check to make sure?"

But she was right, or so the computer assured her.

I burst out laughing. She cracked a rueful smile. "A very popular book," she said.

It was the first time in years I'd had a good laugh with a librarian. Prior visits had been a test of wits – mine – and a test of patience – theirs – as I tried to check out books on their computer or even to remember what I'd come there for. I had been too embarrassed to laugh at anything at all.

⁓

Three weeks passed. I stood in front of the library counter again, returning two books. The same librarian was there, wearing a long Laura Ashley kind of dress with tiny pinkish flowers set against a dark background.

For a moment, she reminded me of a character in a Jane Austen book, until I remembered that Austen's books were set in the Regency period, in the late eighteenth and early nineteenth centuries, while Laura Ashley's original dresses showed a more Victorian influence.

"Good afternoon," I said cheerfully.

The librarian replied as pleasantly as she had the last time.

"Can you tell me, please – what's my number now?"

"Pardon?" She raised her eyebrows, trying to decipher the mystery I had thrown at her.

"My number on the waiting list for *Death Comes to Pemberley*."

"Oh, yes!" She smiled like a co-conspirator and turned to her computer screen again.

"1173," she said.

I rolled my eyes and laughed.

⁓

Roughly two weeks later, I was back in the library, and my favourite librarian was busy doing something librarianish. Trawling the aisles, I headed over to Jane Austen's shelf. But I had already read all of the ones available, including *Northanger Abbey*. So I picked up a Martha Grimes novel instead. Her lead character, Superintendent Richard Jury, is a favourite of mine. So is Jury's good friend Melrose, an English aristocrat who had shed all his titles but not his vast estate.

It occurred to me that reading a murder mystery partly set on a huge English estate would help prepare me for *Death Comes to Pemberley*.

My librarian friend was doing something with a pile of books.

"Hi there!" I called to her, loud enough to get her attention but not break the rules of quietude common to libraries everywhere.

Her eyes lit up. "Would you like me to check for you?"she asked, heading for the computer.

"I'm not sure I should tempt the fates. Do you think I'm any closer to the top of the list?"

"Well, why don't we just find out?"

I agreed, against my better judgment. A person can take only so much disappointment, after all.

"1101!" she declared, almost jubilantly.

"A cause for celebration!" I said.

But, really, who were we kidding? I figured I would spend the rest of my life waiting for it.

~

By then, a sane person might have asked why I didn't just give up and buy the darned thing in a bookstore. But this was not a time for profligate spending. I was going through a period of financial constraints, as Miss Austen might have put it, caused by an extended period of unemployment, caused by the lingering effects of the nasty car accident. (By this, Dear Reader, I mean that the accident was nasty, not the car. Although I am told that it didn't look too hot after the crash.)

~

It became my secret joke with the librarians. After months of asking them about my place on the waiting list, I always got a smile from them whenever I approached their desk.

Our relationship had changed. For years, I had depended on their help, and they had given it kindly. These four women and one man had, perhaps unknowingly, become part of my survival system.

In the years after the accident, I had difficulty walking, talking, even thinking at times. The modern space that housed the library with its many shelves, books, and computers may as well have been a maze the first time I entered it.

When I shuffled toward the library counter and a librarian directed me to a computer to check out a book, I stared at it, then at her, then started to cry.

I couldn't cobble enough thoughts together to check out a book using a computer or even to explain the reason for my failure. Surprisingly, the librarian took it all in stride, as if addle-brained people came to her library every day.

But between my faulty sense of time and the fact that everything took much longer than before the accident, I incurred fines for almost every book I borrowed. The head librarian took matters in her own hands, arranging to get reminders to me a few days before a book was due.

When she suggested I sign up for a library service that helps people with intellectual or perceptual disabilities, I should have accepted, but didn't. That would have meant accepting that I had a damaged brain.

After that, the librarians looked out for me, without making a big deal about it.

And so I became almost as comfortable there as I did at the church I attended. It was familiar territory. The people here knew me, and I knew them.

And I was among old friends. Books.

~

My number was finally called.

Literally.

A librarian phoned me at home to let me know that *Death Comes to Pemberley* was waiting for me on the reserved shelf.

My librarian friend was waiting at the counter when I arrived. She seemed almost as thrilled as I was.

It was a great read. The reviewers were right: P.D. James really did nail Jane Austen's style of writing.

~

Nearly two years after *Death Comes to Pemberley* was released, I was back at the library.

It was a sunny, cool, spring day, and I was bearing a cloth bag with a book for each librarian. I had signed each copy with a message of thanks for their many acts of kindness during my roughest years.

The librarians beamed, and I beamed back. In a small way, my smile tried to tell them, my success in completing this book was partly because of you.

It was by struggling to read books again – over and over – and by listening to audio books, that I had rediscovered my love of words.

~

I didn't know it then, but in the months to come *A Good Home* would take its place on the shelves of libraries both public and private. I would read excerpts of the book in several venues. Some of those shelves, and some of those readings, would be in spaces I treasure: local public libraries.

Chapter Thirteen

The Fountain Pen

The woman approached me, almost shyly.

We were both attending a birthday party for a friend in a small town in southern Ontario. She was clutching a book.

"I really enjoyed your book," she told me, as she held out her copy. She said she found it both moving and meaningful.

My face flushed with self-conscious delight.

In the years since the accident, I had gradually lost all of my confidence. Despite the awards, the "trailblazing," the stories I had written in earlier years, I was not used to praise. I also was not used to being an author; it always surprised me that people were reading and appreciating my book.

The woman asked me to sign her copy. I fumbled around in my handbag until my fingers found a pen. I fished it out, embarrassed to see it was one of those cheap plastic ballpoint affairs, a souvenir from Mike's Mufflers or Judy's Hairdressing Salon or some other place I could not remember visiting.

One of these days, I thought, I really should get a good pen.

I signed the book for the reader, and she took it back, holding it as if it was something precious.

Hamlin and I were seated beside friends Andrew and Karlene. Later, as the four of us strolled out of the building, Andrew turned to me, and asked, "Do you use fountain pens?"

"I used to use them all the time," I replied, taken aback. "I don't know when I stopped."

～

We stopped in at their home to rest awhile before the drive home. To chat about our families. And to see their garden, of course.

"Andrew's garden," Karlene reminded me. "It's entirely his creation."

Andrew is a surgeon. He also plays a mean jazz guitar. And he's an outstanding gardener. Whenever we visited his garden, or even saw pictures of it, our minds were boggled by its beauty and orderliness.

The four of us ambled along the boxwood hedge that snaked through the length of the backyard, defining the sweep and curve of the garden.

We had seen this garden in all seasons. Even in fall and winter, you could see its curves and almost hear its gentle music.

We paused here and there to admire the different shades and texture of leaves, the varying forms of the trees and plants growing there. Rare evergreens and Japanese weeping maples, rhododendrons, dogwoods, and magnolias.

We walked toward a sturdy wooden pergola that supported a vigorous wisteria vine. It had become a running joke between us four: like Andrew and Karlene, we also owned a stubbornly non-blooming wisteria vine.

I had grown to accept ours because we were just average

gardeners, after all. But I suspected it was especially galling for Andrew that, for all his many horticultural talents, he still could not get the darned thing to bloom.

"A master gardener told me she hard-prunes her wisteria on the coldest day in January," I said, expecting this to pass without comment.

Owners of flowerless wisteria vines hear more old wives' tales about how to get their vines to bloom than pregnant women awaiting the birth of their first child.

Karlene looked noncommittal, refusing to give in to hope. But Andrew perked up immediately. "In January!" he said, looking up at his vine thoughtfully.

"Every few winters she puts on her warmest winter coat, gloves, hat, and boots, grabs her pruning shears, heads out to the garden, and does what she calls 'skeleton pruning.' Never fails. She gets tons of blooms the following spring."

Karlene looked only mildly interested.

"I'm thinking we should get her to skeleton prune both our vines next January," I said.

Andrew's eyes took on an avid gleam.

~

We followed our hosts into their house, pausing in their bright, sunlit kitchen.

Minutes later, Andrew emerged from the hallway, holding a beautiful wooden box. He placed it on the kitchen counter and opened it.

It turned out the surgeon-musician-gardener also made pens. Fountain pens. From wood, stone, and other materials. Meticulously assembled. You sensed immediately that, unlike the wisteria vine, these pens would do what they were supposed to do.

Hamlin and I lifted the pens, touched them, felt their

weight. We admired the smoothness of their exterior, the veins in the wood.

Andrew handed one to me. It was a solid dark blue, cool and beautiful to touch.

I gently removed the top of the pen. And then a strange thing happened. Like Marcel Proust's narrator in *Remembrance of Things Past*, who experiences a rush of memories when he bites into a Madeleine cake, one glance at the nib of the pen sent me spinning into a long-forgotten memory.

~

I was in a classroom in the countryside of Jamaica. I was about eight years old. I was sitting at a small wooden desk with an inkwell at the upper right-hand corner.

I was holding a long thin wooden stick with a nib at one end. I dipped the nib in the inkwell, careful to not add another splotch to the several that had already stained the surface of this desk over the years. I could even smell the ink.

"Penmanship," the teacher always called the art of cursive writing. She was a big, tall woman. She stood at the front of the room overseeing her young students' efforts to link their letters on the page clearly, legibly, pleasing to her eyes.

"Sloppy penmanship is a sign of sloppy character!" I heard her say.

But I blocked her out. I was lost in the smooth flow of words across the page. I suddenly felt smart, accomplished, and older than my years. I had practiced the art of cursive writing with a fountain pen and, for the first time, was satisfied with my results.

And I did it all without smudging the page or splotching the desktop.

~

"Perhaps Cynthia would prefer another pen, Andrew," Karlene said, bringing me back to the present.

"No, no!" I said, looking around at the three of them. Gazing back at my gift, I wondered how to explain what had just happened.

I turned to Andrew and thanked him. "It's a lovely gift. It reminded me of my childhood." I paused then added, "And now I'll have a proper pen for signing books!"

Andrew and Karlene looked at my husband and back at me with knowing smiles.

I laughed. "I guess that's the whole point! You saw that cheap old plastic thing I was using and decided to give me a proper pen! Thank you, both."

As we headed home, I clutched my pen the way the reader had clutched her copy of my book.

Chapter Fourteen

My Tightrope, a Bridge

It was late September now. The gardens looked a bit faded, but everything was still green.

An hour north of Toronto, the air was fresh and cool. On a few trees, leaves were turning yellow, pink, or red.

I was in the backseat of a car – I always felt safer there when a passenger – driven by my dear friend Lisa. Beside her was MerriLynn. We were on our way to my first visit with a book club.

These women had a secondary mission: to protect me, watch for warning signals that I was in trouble; make sure I was okay. It was my first time making an author visit without Hamlin or Lauren by my side.

We didn't talk about any of that as we drove. It had been said. Now it was time to enjoy being together, just three girls on a road trip.

Our vehicle sped over bridges that crossed large lakes, their shores lined with evergreen cedar, pine, and spruce. We were in cottage country now, no doubt about it. It felt far away from Toronto, though we had driven only a couple hours.

We talked about all kinds of things. Our families, books, and how lovely it was to be on this drive together.

When I fell quiet, Lisa and MerriLynn let me be. I had propped myself up on a pillow. I was as comfortable as any woman with a bunch of cranky body parts could possibly be in the back of an SUV.

We left the highways behind. The road narrowed, and the trees and bushes seemed only an arm's length from our windows. Up here, red, russet, and yellow leaves prevailed.

~

We turned right on an even narrower lane then down a long driveway toward the lake. We pulled up beside a sprawling two-storey, flat-roofed house that looked like it was built by Frank Lloyd Wright except it was too new. The exterior was clad in dark brown wood; the roofline and doors were trimmed with black.

Our host, Debbie, greeted us immediately.

Amid a flurry of hugs, kisses, and quick comments about the drive, the weather, the house, we dropped our bags on a hallway bench and followed her.

It was a stunningly beautiful interior, a mix of modern and traditional elements.

A large family room with floor-to-ceiling bookshelves was to the left; a big, yet comfy, kitchen and dining area to the right.

Large windows revealed the lake, its surface reflecting the trees that lined its shores.

~

We sat at one end of a massive dark-maple dining table for a late lunch. The tomatoes, radicchio, and almost everything else we ate came from Debbie's expansive garden near the kitchen.

Debbie's ninety-year-old mother, Gladys, who lived with her and her husband, Jim, held us spellbound with stories from her life. They were stories of hardship, stories of survival, and stories of love. As she described the small house she and her husband had first lived in, and the obstacles they overcame, I thought about my own long journey … the obstacles I had already overcome and the ones still facing me.

Gladys was nearing the end of her life. A talented artist now afflicted with a debilitating illness, she struggled to paint a picture these days. But she had not given up on either painting or life.

We rested after lunch. Then Debbie took my travel companions and me for a walk to the dock, and through the woods. The three of them walked slowly, looking back occasionally and calling, "You okay, Cynthia?"

I was indeed.

Late September. Not the best time for a swim in the lake, but the very best time for a walk in the woods along the shoreline. No mosquitoes, no deer flies. Just the trees, the call of birds, occasional glimpses of the lake, and the soft crunch of our footsteps.

~

In a few hours, it was evening.

We were joined by a steady stream of visitors: members of Debbie's Limberlost Book Club. Most of the women lived along this lake or others nearby, but a few had driven in from nearby towns and villages.

Soon it would be my turn to tell and read stories, about the homes I had lived in, the generations of my family, the experiences they and I had shared. As I slowly moved around the large room introducing myself, I was greeted with a friendly smile and a "Hi, Cynthia!"

Of course: they'd seen my photo on the back cover of the book. They already knew who I was.

~

It was my first time with a group of people who had already read my book, and I decided to try something new. Before reading an excerpt to them, before making any comments, I asked the group to share their reactions to the memoir.

The women's responses were spontaneous and warm. They talked about the homes in the book, their favourite characters and events, and the universal themes of childhood, whether in Jamaica or Canada.

It was a lively give-and-take between my intentions as an author and their reactions as readers. We shared thoughts about reflection, redemption, recovery.

I had to remind myself to stay on guard, to watch the direction of my thoughts. But I knew that, if worse came to worst, I'd be supported. By Lisa, MerriLynn, Debbie, Gladys, and every other woman there.

Once in a while, for a few precious moments, I felt safe: my tightrope had turned into a wide bridge.

Chapter Fifteen

Kicking Pain in the Teeth

Jamaicans have a saying for every situation. One of my favourites is: "You haffe tek bad tings mek joke." *Sometimes things get so bad you have to make a joke out of them.*

The therapists at the rehabilitation hospital had tried to teach me that laughter can help healing, but I was having none of it. Laughter seemed trivial in such dire circumstances. I was too serious, too angry, to laugh.

I don't remember when I started to laugh again.

It may have been when I started to realize that chronic pain is a bore: never-ending, monotonous, bleak. At its worst, it is excruciating, blasting away all sensible thought, all fighting spirit, twisting you, beating you, smashing you to smithereens.

It may have been when Jane, an elderly friend, called me several times in one week and I finally understood: she had recognized the despair in my voice and was worried.

Or it may have been when my friend Muriel, the octo-genarian artist, was having a tough time after a series of operations that left her in pain. I remember deciding to make her laugh at least once per phone conversation.

It also may have been when, on my most painful days,

I started writing crazy poems in my notebook and shared them with readers of the blog I'd recently started. A single word at first; then a whole line; then I'd try to find words for a second line that rhymed. It was silly and nonsensical, and when my readers laughed, I laughed, too.

I don't know when I started to laugh. But I did, and the Toronto Rehab therapists were right: it was a good thing.

~

Once a month, in spring and summer, I met Arna and Phyllis, always at the same restaurant in a suburban mall.

I never would have met these women were it not for the times we spent as outpatients in the same program at Toronto Rehab, trying to come to terms with constant pain, trying to figure out alternatives to narcotic painkillers.

An onlooker might have expected us to be miserable, and sometimes we were. We admitted to those times when the pain had all but got us beat. In fact, these women were among the few people in the world I could always tell the miserable truth.

We never had to pretend with each other. We had tried, and it hadn't worked. We could even tell from each other's voices on the phone.

When I talked to other graduates of the Toronto Rehab program, it wasn't unusual for one of us to ask, "Seriously, how are you really feeling today?" and for the other person to admit, with a long sigh, "The truth is that it's been a really crappy week. The pain's been very, very bad."

We understood these things better than most.

But, as Arna reminded us, "I might be in pain, but I don't have to *be* a pain."

And so we laughed. Perhaps the most surprising thing is how much laughing we did on our lunch dates. That certainly was true of my first trio, with Arna and Phyllis, and of my second, with Penny and Joan. Penny had the ability to crack Joan and me up with one short sentence. The woman was a born comic.

"Why don't you write comedy?" I asked her almost every time we met.

"Because it's just stuff I say. I don't even know it's funny till someone laughs."

It's as if we had all made a pledge to find the ridiculous in the pain that hounded us. Or perhaps we realized that each of us suffered enough misery when we were alone so we might as well laugh when we were together.

We laughed at the silliest things. Maybe that was because we gave each other licence to say the silliest things to each other.

One day, Arna and I both noticed that Phyllis seemed especially anxious. It turned out she was feeling intense pain, her allergies were acting up, and she was pushing herself extra hard to complete certain tasks.

"You need to rest," Arna said.

Phyllis' reply was immediate. "I'm too tired to rest."

"You're too tired to rest?"

The three of us laughed so hard it's a wonder we didn't choke on our food.

Chronic pain never stops; that's why they call it chronic. Only the severity fluctuates.

Sunny, cool, dry days are helpful to some people. Wet, cold, humid days are agony to many. And freezing temperatures? Extreme cold does a number not just on our bodies but also on our minds.

We learned several drug-free, pain-fighting techniques at Toronto Rehab. When we got together, we shared the ones we had tried lately: which ones helped this time, which ones didn't.

The act of staying in touch and of keeping this

commitment to regular lunches were just two of the tools we used to fight back against depression and despair, chronic pain's travelling companions.

And when we laughed at the truly ridiculous things one of us said on a day when even the act of walking was painful, we weren't just using a tool we had learned. Pain kicked us in the butt every day; kicking it in the teeth once a month was the very least we could do.

Chapter Sixteen

Looking PTSD in the Eye

I couldn't move if my life depended on it.

There, on the radio, was a man talking about his struggle with PTSD.

I wanted to turn it off, but couldn't. I sat at the kitchen table, listening.

~

He described his nightmares.

"Night visions," he called them. Always, they involve terrible danger. Always, the danger is to the people he loves. Always, he watches, helpless.

He finally wakes up, drenched with sweat. Unable to move. The small tasks of daily living are mountainous obstacles in the hours and days after. Even dressing himself requires a mighty struggle.

~

How did this stranger know?

Here was my private struggle, shared only with my therapists, doctors, and immediate family, now aired for anyone to hear.

I wept. For him, for me, and for many others.

PTSD: the silent struggle of so many. Returning

soldiers. Earthquake and hurricane survivors Police officers and firefighters. Countless individuals who have experienced violent attacks, or– as in my case – car accidents. All struggling to return to a normal life. Most keeping silent about the hard truths of daily living.

~

I woke up, startled by something I couldn't remember. Didn't want to remember.

I shook my head, trying to clear it, trying to rid myself of the remnants of the nightmare, forcing myself to think of something cheerful. My daughters. My husband. The flowers in my garden.

Hamlin was upstairs in our bedroom, and I downstairs on the sofa. I had exiled myself from the bedroom earlier in the week, after frightening him from a deep sleep yet again. I'd been having a deep sleep, too – the kind that brings on the night terrors.

As we had our coffee early the morning after the first nightmare, I had tried to make a joke of it. "Remember when the screams that came from our bedroom were shouts of laughter or, even better, passion?"

Hamlin had smiled a little, but said nothing.

By night three, I couldn't find anything funny about the situation. I had grabbed two pillows and an old quilt and headed downstairs.

The nightmares kept on coming, night after night. But at least I wasn't disturbing Hamlin.

~

Awake, a person who has PTSD is always vigilant, always monitoring her thoughts. Asleep, it's much worse. Either way, there's no running from it, only painstaking efforts to manage it. It – and the constant pain that disrupts and bedevils everything.

Part Two

Taking to the Verandah

Chapter Seventeen

Sharing the Harvest

It was a few days before Thanksgiving Day, October 2013, and the harvest was in. One of my mother's sayings came to my mind: "You don't have to be rich to plant a garden."

No matter how little money our families had, my mother always planted one. Same with Hamlin's mother, Merle, and his sister Fay, who grew abundant produce and flowers in a small plot behind their home in mid-Toronto.

In Hamlin's herb garden behind the farmhouse, everything was thriving. Chives, tarragon, oregano, basil. Thyme and rosemary. Lemon balm. Summer savoury. And mint – plenty of mint: apple mint, black mint, spearmint.

Our vegetable garden had yielded abundantly this year: eggplants, beans, peppers, onions, zucchini, cucumber. And a profusion of tomatoes.

In a fit of late-in-the-day ambition, the pumpkin vine even flowered again and put out several perfect tiny pumpkins.

The vine was Jamaican pumpkin, grown from a seedling that came from neighbours Paddy and Jacqui. Only one of its pumpkins made it to maturity this summer, and now, in early October, the intrepid vine was trying again.

I thanked it for the effort, but warned that it was indulging in a lost cause.

"You're in Canada now," I told it – one of the foolish things I tended to say to plants and shrubs when I walked through the garden. "Cold weather is just around the corner."

But last time I checked, the vine had sent out yet another flower, atop yet another tiny pumpkin.

We were thankful for the one mature pumpkin it gave us, and decided to treat it like a whole crop. So we called Paddy and Jacqui to come for their share of "the pumpkin harvest."

"What about the bird pepper I gave you?" Jacqui asked as she came through the kitchen door.

"It got overshadowed by the asparagus and raspberry bushes," Hamlin said. "We realized too late. It's just blooming now."

"But the raspberry bushes you gave us a few years ago are on their second or third yield this summer," I chimed in, wanting to atone for our inept treatment of the bird pepper plant, not to mention our failure to get more than one mature pumpkin.

Along with one half of the pumpkin, we gave Jacqui and Paddy tomatoes, herbs, and garlic. They were happy with their share of the harvest.

The garlic bulbs were yanked out of the soil in late summer and left to dry in baskets and boxes. The biggest ones were given to family and friends like Paddy and Jacqui, the smaller ones left behind for our own use.

~

The two large old apple trees in our back garden bore thousands of fruit every other year. In their off year, however, they still bore hundreds.

The apples gleamed between and through the green

leaves surrounding them. Patches of red, mingled with splashes of pink and yellow. A heritage apple, Wolf River, they were as big as grapefruit, yet fragrant; sweet, yet tart.

The trees were never sprayed with chemicals, so some of the apples had worms. Several fell every day, some suffering small bruises as they dropped onto the thick soft grass below. They weren't the ones we gave to neighbours and friends. But they were perfect for making jelly and pies. I simply cut around the worms or bruises.

~

Around the perimeter of our grounds, the maple leaves were deep yellow, some already turning red.

They were drifting, falling, settling. On the lawns, driveway, and sidewalk. A glorious mess, perfect for dogs and small children – or adults with a sense of fun – to play in.

Inside, the house glowed with warmth. Wooden floors burnished with the patina of age. These floors had seen many feet, many families, many autumns.

The furniture – tables, chairs, the old hutch, the bookshelves – glowed in the late-day sunshine. The rays landed on the harvest table in the kitchen as it relived the glory of previous harvests, previous bounties, previous lives.

Hamlin brought this table home shortly after we bought our first house together. Made of thick maple slabs, eight feet long, it once stood in the kitchen of a Masonic hall.

At one end of the table, full of fresh produce from our garden, was a double-sided basket like the ones you see on a donkey in pictures of old-time Jamaican country living.

My mother had given me this basket, decades ago. It lived on top of a kitchen cupboard except when pressed into duty in the late summer and autumn.

The rest of the harvest table was covered with apple

pies and jars of apple jelly, the sight kindling memories of autumn days past.

Bert, the grandson of the people who built this house, a tall, friendly man now in his eighties, brought us an old apple pie dish his mother used several decades before. It had a white enamel surface rimmed with red and a single chip on the bottom.

We were fond of this man and fond of that old plate with its chip. Impressed by its survival, we gave it pride of place in our cupboard.

Earlier on this day, I stood at the stove, peering inside a huge pot, watching the apple jelly bubble inside.

It didn't matter how many times I had already done this, I was never sure if it would gel. When it did, I acknowledged the miracle with a childish yell of triumph.

On the other side of our country kitchen, Hamlin stood at the harvest table, rolling out the dough, wondering if it would be light enough, flaky enough, or too much of both. He was trying a gluten-free dough for the first time and was as anxious about its success as I was about the jelly.

The smell of apples and cinnamon, apples and mint – apples, apples, glorious apples – reminded me of the autumns when our children were small and loved being passed pieces of apple as I sliced. Sometimes I'd chant, "One for you, two for me" – meaning two for the bowl. Or their father would allow them to lick the bowl after he'd scooped out the mixture of sliced apples, mushed pears, cinnamon, nutmeg, sugar, and a bit of lemon juice.

The children were grown-ups now, with their own homes, their own lives. But the scent of apples, cinnamon, and mint in the fall always brought back the memories, of people and times loved.

I smiled at Hamlin and he smiled back. We were sharing the same memory.

"I am happy!" I said. "Let it be remembered, when I am old and grey, that on this day, I was gloriously, completely happy!"

Hamlin refocused his eyes on the pastry, but I sensed he was listening intently. And wanting to appear less moved than I knew he was.

He didn't look up at me. He said only, "Hm-hmm?"

"Hm-hmmm," I replied.

Chapter Eighteen

The Matriarch and the Uncle

My great-aunt Rose was on my mind.

I wished I could visit her in New Jersey, but couldn't. Pain and lack of sleep had worn me down. Dr. Helen, on my recent visit, had noted that I was in relapse. She had told me to go home and "stay there." There was to be no more book-related work.

I had no choice but to obey.

Lying in bed, during those days, my mind frequently turned to Aunt Rose, whose health was declining. I owed her so much, I thought. She was one of the people closest to me, and a constant source of love, encouragement, and prayers.

She had also been close to my mother and grand-mother: aunt to one, sister to the other. She had outlived them both and, with our loving approval, had become the de facto matriarch of our family.

She had mourned the loss of her older sister, my grandmother Artress, who had played a special role in her life. But the death that rocked her to her core was more recent. It was that of her niece – my mother, Louise – who died the same year I had the accident.

These two had been almost as close as mother and

daughter. Across the decades and oceans that later separated them, many letters flew between these women, sharing news of their lives, keeping them connected.

Even when my mother Louise was in her late seventies, Aunt Rose still called her "Girlie." There was a world of feeling behind that word.

When her beloved Girlie died, Aunt Rose's grief was transformed into caring for us children. She telephoned us often, warming our hearts with her concern for us and memories of our mother.

Over those years, we talked about many different things, almost all of them related to our family's history.

"How come you and Mama were so close, Aunt Rose?" I asked one day.

"Didn't I tell you this before?" Her tone said she had but it had fallen through my sieve of a brain.

"Well," she began, "I was living with my sister and her husband – your grandparents – when your mother was born. I was right there from the day Girlie was born, Dahling. I was one of the first people to hold her in my arms. I loved her right then. We always kept in close touch. We never, ever lost touch, Dahling."

"I know, Aunt Rose. She loved you, too, very much."

After the pause that always followed a mention of my mother, I asked, "Where did my grandparents live back then, Aunt Rose?"

"In a little house with a verandah. Up on the hill near the Salvation Army church near Mandeville. It was a rented house, you know, Dahling. They were a young couple back then."

I had not known about this house. Nor that Aunt Rose, and younger sister Lyn, had lived with them.

Most of the land in our family's district had once been owned by my grandfather Victor's family. By the time I was born, all of it had been split up and passed on to their many descendants. Some of those descendants had become land rich, and many were educated, but, overall, the family had become cash poor.

My grandparents' house, the house where my immediate family had lived for nearly ten years, was on one of the bigger parcels of family land.

"What was my grandfather like, Aunt Rose? He is such a legend in the family because of his brilliance ... and those inventions of his. I wish I'd met him. Pity he died so long before I was born."

"Your grandfather Victor was a very handsome man, Dahling. You never saw any pictures of him?"

"I never did, Aunt Rose."

"Well, his family was mixed – some were black people and some were white people from England. He came out looking kind of Indian, with straight hair and a straight nose. He was descended from a wealthy, aristocratic family, you know ... but I told you that already."

As always, I was scribbling, trying to capture every word.

"He was a brilliant man, Dahling. He had a very quick mind. He used to perform at concerts, you know. Telling stories and making up riddles. No one could ever figure out the answers to those riddles."

"But he had his jewelry shop, and was always inventing something. How did he find time to go around performing?"

"You find time, Dahling. When you have a lot of children, you don't turn down money. He was paid to perform, you know. Oh yes, he was in demand for his riddles. No one could ever guess the answers."

My mother used to tell us about her father and how he enthralled local crowds. All nine children had inherited their storytelling talent from him.

And Grandfather Victor invented, among other things,

a vehicle that could hold several passengers. It looked so unusual that the authorities would not give him a licence to drive it on the road.

⁓

Talks with Aunt Rose often went like this, with one answer leading to a memory of something I had heard but forgotten, another leading to a surprising bit of family history.

She remembered minute details. From decades, even a hundred years ago.

"Did I ever tell you about the time when …"

Sometimes the memories came complete with dialogue and tiny details such as the style of a dress or shoes that someone wore.

Hamlin and I were impressed with her quick recall and ready answers.

"What do you think was the single most important invention in your lifetime?" Hamlin asked her one day. He thought she would say the airplane or telephone or some such thing.

"The light bulb!"

"Why?"

"It lengthened the day. Before that you had to go to bed very early. There's only so much you could do by candle or lamplight. Because of the light bulb, you could read after dark."

⁓

This time, that November, it was her daughter, True, who called, telling me that Aunt Rose, recently returned from the hospital and bedridden for weeks now, seemed to be preparing to die. She held the phone for Aunt Rose.

"Dahling?"

"Hi, my dear Aunt Rose." I tried to make my voice

sound normal, but I was filled with dread at the thought of her passing.

"I'm so proud of you," she said.

"You are?"

"I just finished reading your book."

"Oh ..." Tears sprang to my eyes. "I didn't know you'd read it, Aunt Rose."

"Someone read it to me," she said in a weak voice. "It's a very good book, you know, Dahling. And I want you to promise me something."

"Yes, Aunt Rose?"

"Promise me you'll write another one. You have to write a second book."

I hesitated. Her voice had weakened again as she spoke those last few words, but I sensed she was waiting for my response.

The trouble is that I had never lied to Aunt Rose and wasn't about to start then. What if I never wrote another book? I would have broken the last promise I'd made to her.

"I'll try, Aunt Rose."

Her voice was suddenly stronger. "No! That's not good enough, Dahling. You have a God-given talent. Trying is not good enough."

"Okay, Aunt Rose. I'll do my best." I was hedging my bets, trying to make this sound like a promise without technically being a promise.

Aunt Rose wasn't fooled. She laughed gently and said, "I know you will."

She died later that month.

~

Mama's younger brother Gerald, who lived in London, England, had also been close to Aunt Rose. After my mother died, their mutual loss made their friendship even more precious.

"He's like a son to her," True told me once.

Aunt Rose could never rely on me to call regularly. My brain didn't work that way. Uncle Gerald, however, never let her down. He called her at least once a week.

They both loved sharing family stories, and they loved to banter.

I was told that, in the weeks leading to Aunt Rose's death, Uncle Gerald called her even more often. I don't know what they said to each other, but I know they would have shared loving words, and Gerald might even have shared a joke.

I thought about him often during those weeks. I felt he was better prepared for her death than the rest of us were. Still, my sisters and I wondered if he'd be able to cope when she died.

~

"I'm sorry, Uncle G," I said by phone after I received news of Aunt Rose's death. "I know how much you will miss her."

His voice didn't betray any emotion. "But she had a good innings, didn't she?" he said.

So typical of my British uncles to use a cricket term to describe a long life.

"Well, she batted well over a century," I replied. "Just three months shy of a hundred and eight."

"Ah, my dear, that's something to be very glad for, isn't it?"

"Yes, Uncle G. It is."

He was keeping a stiff upper lip, but I was still concerned about him. With Aunt Rose gone, he had lost the last link to his parents. And though we younger ones tried to fill the gap, we had not lived in those early times.

We had not shared in the events that he and his beloved aunt so often discussed. At times it was as if we spoke different languages.

I wished I were there to hug him now, to be there when he missed Aunt Rose and wanted to talk. But our large Jamaican family had chosen migration decades earlier and were split up across North America, Britain, and Jamaica.

Uncle Gerald and I were separated by oceans – one consisting of water, the other of memories.

~

Uncle Gerald's favourite pastime, next to playing dominoes with his brothers, Jack and Eddie, was to take the bus on long journeys to places in England and Wales that he had heard about in his decades of living there but never had a chance to visit. Long retired and living on a pension, he now had the time to travel.

"Where did you go this time, Uncle G?" my sisters and I asked whenever we called him. We urged him to share the details of his destination, whether city, town, village, or the seaside.

Or he told us about taking the bus to brother Eddie's house, where his sister-in-law Madge made them all a nice meal, and the three brothers played dominoes.

Every Christmas Day, we, his nieces and nephew, knew we could speak to all three brothers and Aunt Madge simply by calling Uncle Eddie's home. They passed the phone from one to the other, and, by the time I had talked to all three, I had heard three different jokes.

They were a funny bunch, these brothers. Another talent inherited from their father, Victor.

~

The months after Aunt Rose's death were tough ones for Uncle Gerald, in a way we didn't expect.

His legs stopped working. His arms were inflamed. No more travel to far-flung destinations in Britain. This independent man who had never married became more and more dependent on others as the paralysis spread. Doctors could not explain the source of his illness.

For a while, his condition seemed to become worse each day. The thought that his illness was psychosomatic – perhaps caused by grief – was soon dismissed. Whatever this was, it was serious.

Across the ocean, our anxiety grew.

Our uncles Eddie and Jack and Jack's children Norma and Carl updated us on his condition. We were grateful. Uncle G had been a blessing to my siblings and me. He had consoled and comforted us in those awful days, weeks, and months after our mother had died of a stroke, and he kept in touch with us often.

I suspected he and Aunt Rose had made a pledge to keep us supported throughout the ordeal of our loss. We loved them for it.

But now Uncle Gerald was at a loss, and there seemed very little we could do except murmur words of comfort on the telephone. We consoled and encouraged him throughout his time in the hospital. We consoled him when he was forced to move from his upstairs flat – the one with the great view of London – to a ground-floor flat in a different area.

But we could not give him what he wanted most – to walk again, to be independent again – nor could we be my mother or Aunt Rose for him.

Then one day, my friend Mandy sent me a link to a song I had heard in our house over and over again during my childhood. I remembered hearing it on the radio and sung or hummed by my mother as she went about her chores. The song was written by Septimus Winner in 1868 and became popular in 1949, just four years after the end of the Second World War. My mother was in her early twenties, and Uncle Gerald was a teenager. Surely he would know it.

~

I had planned to call him the next day.

That night, as I sat at my computer, the phone rang.

"Uncle Gerald!" I said. "You beat me to it again! I planned to call you early tomorrow morning!"

"Ah, Miss Hya," he said, using a childhood pet name few people knew. "I was concerned when you didn't call back. I thought maybe your health had gotten worse."

I felt guilty as I inquired about his health. "Any improvement in walking?" I asked.

"I use two canes to get around sometimes, but still can't walk on my own."

"Uncle G," I murmured sympathetically.

"What can we do, my dear? It's life, isn't it?"

"Yes, Uncle G."

And then I remembered to ask him if he knew the song "Whispering Hope."

"Yes, of course. I still know all the words."

"Shall we sing it together?"

"Of course, my dear."

Then he in his flat in London and I in my office in the farmhouse sang the first two verses together.

Soft as the voice of an angel,
Breathing a lesson unheard,
Hope with a gentle persuasion
Whispers her comforting word:
Wait till the darkness is over,
Wait till the tempest is done,
Hope for the sunshine tomorrow,
After the shower is gone.

Whispering hope, oh, how welcome thy voice,
Making my heart in its sorrow rejoice.

If, in the dusk of the twilight
Dim be the region afar,
Will not the deepening darkness
Brighten the glimmering star?
Then when the night is upon us,
Why should the heart sink away?
When the dark midnight is over
Watch for the breaking of day.

Whispering hope, oh, how welcome thy voice,
Making my heart in its sorrow rejoice.

His voice was melodious, mine a bit wobbly, but I didn't stutter even once. My heart swelled in my chest, my face wore a foolish smile.

When the song ended, we bade each other goodnight.

I had recently said my last goodbye to Aunt Rose, but, thankfully, this was not my last to Uncle G.

Chapter Nineteen

Each Season Brings a Gift

One day that autumn, after being ill in bed for several days, I looked around at our small bedroom and decided it needed sprucing up. The old white cotton duvet cover looked pristine over the white sheets on our bed, but together they suddenly looked sterile to me..

I was still living by the rule of making do with what you have, so I rummaged around in the bedrooms until I found two old white shams in the back of a cupboard. Their cotton lace edges were so perky, they made me smile. I used them to cover two of the pillows at the head of our bed. Then, for a splash of colour, I carefully positioned a charming red-and-white cushion in front of them.

Across the room, on the window seat, I placed the matching cushion. Years ago, I'd been given these cushions and loved them because of the white snowflakes and red reindeer they bore. It was a nod to Christmas, which was still several weeks away, but I thought it a cheerful scene. I could hardly wait for Hamlin to see what I'd done.

He went to bed before me that night. The next morning, I asked brightly: "What did you think of the way I decorated our bedroom?"

"Decorated?" he asked.

"Yes."

He actually scratched his head then looked at me quizzically.

"Didn't you notice anything different?"

"Oh! You mean ... all those pillows and stuff?"

I nodded.

"I didn't really look at them. I was tired. I had to throw them off the bed before going to sleep ... I hope you don't mind."

I suppressed the urge to throw a cushion at him and went to peer over his side of the bed. There, in the corner, on the floor, were the pillows and cushion, looking quite forlorn.

"You're just lucky I love you," I said, shaking my head.

But he looked like a small boy, contrite over a misdemeanour.

Before I could stop myself, I started smiling.

~

Each season brought its own gifts: there was always something we could use to decorate the inside or outside of the house.

In the cold months, I started with what was already inside. I switched freshly laundered bedspreads from one room to another; polished furniture with beeswax; and changed the tablecloth in the dining room. I placed white candles in candlesticks on the table in the dining room or hallway.

Family photos and other wall hangings changed places in some rooms; since I still had limited movement in my neck and arm I asked my good man to help me move the bigger pictures on the walls.

He obliged, all the while claiming he didn't quite understand why I couldn't "just leave the stuff alone," and sometimes declaring, with a twinkle in his eyes, that "the old way looked better to me."

I pretended not to hear him, pursing my lips to hide my smile.

The old Hudson's Bay blanket – with thick stripes in yellow, red, green, and blue – was used as a throw on a bed or armchair, providing instant cheer wherever it found itself. One side showed a pale stain, the reason it was reduced to only twenty dollars in an antiques shop in small-town Ontario. I always pretended the stain was artwork.

In autumn, when the flower garden had died down, I looked to the shrubs for colour and rediscovered that the philosopher Albert Camus was right: autumn is indeed "a second spring when every leaf is a flower." When placed in a vase on a table indoors, branches of the tall ninebark shrub with their plum-coloured leaves were as lovely as flowers.

In winter, the dogwood shrub at the back of the garden provided an abundance of upright red canes for sticking in tall containers on the verandah near the front door.

Cones fell from the pine and spruce trees. We used some to fill a glass bowl and a pretty basket. Decorations for the Christmas tree came from boxes in our basement, but the greenery on the mantel, doors, and tabletops came from evergreen trees and shrubs outside.

We cut evergreen branches – cedar, euonymus, boxwood, spruce, and pine – to fill vases and clay pots or create boughs, tying them together with a shiny red ribbon to hang on doors.

In spring, we placed daffodils, tulips, and sprigs of pretty blue forget-me-nots or fragrant lily of the valley in mason jars in our bedrooms.

Our somewhat plain dining room suddenly felt elegant when tall, arching fronds of Solomon's seal or pink blousy peony flowers were placed in a vase in the centre of the bare wooden table.

Come the summer and we had an abundance of flowers to choose from: lilies in many colours, from a creamy pink to a dark yellow and a shade I called flushed peach, having lost the label long ago; deeply fragrant pink roses; red bee balm; white Annabelle hydrangea.

From early spring to the end of summer, I knew what it was to be rich. I was wealthy in flowers, and that was a wondrous thing to be.

~

A strange thing happened in this period of my life. At the same time that I was learning to make my surroundings more satisfying by making do with the simple gifts around me, I was also developing a laissez-faire attitude toward entertaining.

Not that we did much of that, but on the few occasions when we did entertain, I felt insecure about myself and anxious about the house.

I woke up one day and realized I had stopped caring about what visitors thought of my house. As I wrote to a friend: "As long as the house is clean, as long as there are fresh sheets and flowers from my garden in the guest room, and people have enough to eat, I feel great. I don't worry about impressing anyone, and I only invite people I like to my home. But this attitude didn't happen overnight. It took years."

Chapter Twenty

A Precious Hour

I had slept for almost two hours this time, and that, in my world, was a lot of sleep.

In the bedroom next door, Julius' snoring sounded like a freight train. I couldn't figure out how a dog that small could produce such an enormous snore.

I heard movement. A few minutes later, I heard it again. Quietly, gingerly, so as not to disturb my sleeping husband, I got out of bed, my feet feeling for my slippers on the floor in the darkness, my hand reaching for the robe I had thrown across my dresser before getting in bed. I headed next door.

"Lauren," I said softly from the hallway, "are you awake?"

Our younger daughter and her two little dogs were spending the weekend with us.

"Yes."

"I'm going downstairs to make some herbal tea to help me sleep. Want some?"

"Sure! Thanks."

She took the long maple staircase at the front of the house. I took the back staircase down to the kitchen. I moved slowly those days, and by the time I got there,

Lauren already had the electric kettle plugged in and was rooting around in the pantry.

"I'm hungry," she said. "I haven't eaten since supper at five o'clock yesterday evening."

It was nearly three o'clock on Saturday morning.

I smiled mischievously at her. "Want some apple crumble?"

"Yesss!" she replied, closing the pantry door, a big smile on her face.

In one super-swift step, she was in front of the fridge and holding a can of whipped cream.

In for a penny, in for a pound, my mother would have said. If we were going to have apple pie at three in the morning, we might as well have whipped cream on it, too.

We sat companionably at the harvest table in the kitchen, door firmly closed so we wouldn't disturb Hamlin.

Our farmhouse kitchen was surrounded by a verandah on three sides. During the day, light shone in through its windows and the upper glass panes of three doors. At times like this, however, the room was bathed in soft light, surrounded by the darkness outside.

One curly lock kept escaping Lauren's hair clasp and straying down her caramel-coloured cheek. It made her look more like a teenager than a young woman in her twenties.

"How come you can't sleep?" I asked.

"Because I went to bed at seven. I was so tired, I went to bed too early. Then Julius' snoring woke me up. It wasn't like a short snort, or anything like that. I swear: that dog snored for about fifteen minutes straight. It's so loud!"

"He seems to be snoring even louder these days. Is he?"

"Yes, he is. It's allergy season for him."

"Oh." If I knew dogs got allergies, I had forgotten.

"I don't mind if he snores after I fall asleep. But if

I have to lie there and listen to him snore, it's really hard to get to sleep."

She imitated the offending dog's snoring with remarkable accuracy. We both burst out laughing.

We sipped our tea and tucked into the pie, and it seemed to me that tea and apple pie had never tasted so good.

"How much sleep did you get?" she asked me.

"I was lucky. I got about two hours before the pain woke me up."

"Two hours. How do you do that? I couldn't do it."

"I'm almost used to it. Except for when it goes on for too many nights and I find myself stuttering, unable to think or speak clearly during the day. That's frustrating."

"It's just exhaustion, Mom." Her brown eyes implored me to believe. "I know it freaks you out when it happens, and then you start thinking your head injury has gotten worse. But I've noticed the stuttering's worse when you're exhausted and worrying. Stop worrying."

Her words were as comforting as a warm embrace.

Normally, I was the only person awake at this time, alone in the darkness with pain racking my injured limbs and remnants of a nightmare taunting my mind. Sometimes the pain medication worked for a few hours. Sometimes, I got comfort from silent prayers and meditation. Most times, I got out of bed and exercised for a while then headed to the computer and wrote.

But some nights, nothing worked. My truant thoughts strayed from the night terrors into the other danger zone of my uncertain future and lingered there too long. And then came the sense of being utterly alone, a feeling at once engulfing and hollowing and almost worse than the pain.

So, while I wanted my daughter to get her sleep, it was a joy to have her with me at this wee hour of the morning.

Just then we heard a gentle scratching on the other side of the kitchen door.

"Julius ..." Lauren said knowingly. Of course it was Julius. It would take a firecracker to rouse Dawson, the older dog, this time of the morning.

I opened the door, and Julius bounded through. He was fourteen pounds of energy, with short dark brown hair and a bright eyed, intelligent-looking little face, all atop four thin legs. When he ran, it was as if his legs had a life of their own.

"Want to go outside?" Lauren asked him.

He made for the mudroom door.

We turned on the outside lights so Julius could see where he was going. On impulse, I donned a light coat over my night robe, put on my walking shoes, grabbed my cane, and headed outside to be with him.

The air was fresh and cold. A full moon lit up the garden, illuminating the shapes of the giant hosta leaves and making each plant and shrub seem twice as large as in the daylight. On many a sleepless night I had thought of walking around the garden, but I had never done so until now.

Julius peed against a low bush and accompanied me on my slow walkabout. Or maybe I was accompanying him. We meandered companionably until it was time to go back inside.

"Did you know it's a full moon?" I asked Lauren once back in the kitchen.

"Yes."

"Maybe that's why you can't sleep."

"No. I just went to bed way too early. I was tired. That and the snoring."

She put our plates and forks into the dishwasher as we talked. We each dropped our teabag into the compost bucket under the kitchen sink and put the cups in the dishwasher, too.

As Lauren and Julius headed back upstairs, I wished them a good sleep.

"You, too, Mom."

I reached for a notebook and pen and wrote about the moments I had just spent with my daughter. I wrote quickly, and then I wrote some more.

Finally I went upstairs to bed – quietly, quietly, so as not to interrupt Hamlin's sleep. This beloved man had been through so much since the accident, I couldn't stand to cause him even the slightest bit of hardship. I gently shifted and turned in the bed, hoping to find a position that would allow me to fall asleep before the sun rose.

Maybe I would get another hour's sleep. Or two.

Maybe. And maybe not.

But it had been a precious hour, one I would not have missed for all the tea in China.

Chapter Twenty-one

Mighty Dawson

Dawson flew through the open door from the verandah, ears and tail flapping, a speeding bundle of white fur.

I watched him, holding my breath. Sometimes I even closed my eyes. This small dog – a Havanese – still seemed so vulnerable that I never became accustomed to his mighty race through the house after a short walk outside in the garden.

Through the mudroom, through the kitchen, through the long hallway he charged. Then a sharp turn to the left at the last second and through the long living room, barely missing some of the furniture.

Hamlin called it Dawson's Victory Lap, but I called it the mad dash.

This is the time he's going to crash into that table leg or the edge of that open door or the large coffee table in the centre of the living room, I would think, cringing.

And, indeed, it happened once or twice when he didn't make the turn fast enough. But somehow, despite his speed, despite his hair flapping over his eyes, he made it without mishap – then came back to the kitchen and did it all over again.

Dinner was waiting in his bowl in one corner of the kitchen. As he walked purposefully toward the bowl, he seemed to smile, giddy with joy.

How could we not feel a sense of wonder and delight at this small dog? Abandoned, dehydrated, and worn out when our daughter first found him, he had taken a while to get used to us. But, cared for by Lauren, then by the whole family, Dawson found his forever home.

~

I always loved my children's pets.

Nikisha and Tim had two cats. Jerome, the large ginger-haired one, strode through the house with a swagger of extreme confidence. Simon, his brother cat, was the very opposite: brindle-haired, he liked to hide in closets and, for days at a time, emerged only long enough to eat and perform his ablutions.

Lauren had two dogs: Julius, a brown-black mixture of pug and chihuahua, and Dawson, her little rescue dog of indeterminate age. We figured he was about ten years old when Lauren found him, but not even the vet would hazard a "firm guess."

Dawson, except when he rushed in from a very short walk outside, was slow and plodding. Head down, he moved carefully. He occasionally bumped into a wall or got lost under the furniture and had to be gently hauled out.

This dog kept his own counsel and seemed to live in a world of his own. He couldn't do long walks outside; he tired easily. He didn't engage much with others; his memory seemed poor and he occasionally seemed lost. When we took him in for treatment, the vet always looked on him with a mix of pity and bemusement.

Perhaps that's why I empathized with this little dog so much. He sometimes reminded me of myself.

~

On the way home one day from my Saturday-morning therapy, I had spied the little white dog, head down, walking slowly but steadily on the sidewalk. He reminded me of a little old man who knew exactly where he was going and refused to be distracted.

I slowed the car and followed him for a few long blocks, hoping he would veer off the sidewalk toward one of the adjacent homes. He didn't.

I followed him some more then stopped, got out of the car, and approached him. He turned and raced off in the opposite direction. I didn't stand a chance of catching him. I made it back to my car, and drove home.

It was Easter weekend and there was much on my mind: taking the hand bells to church for ringing at the end of the Sunday service; making sure we had everything we needed for family dinner; tidying up the house; making sure the powder room was clean.

It was a full half hour before I remembered the little white dog. I told Lauren what had happened.

"Mom!" she said, jumping to her feet. "We have to go look for him."

"I'm sure he's back home by now."

"But we don't know that. What if it was one of our dogs? Wouldn't you want someone to help him?"

So off we went, with Julius in the back seat. We drove around and around till Lauren spotted a teenage boy bending over something under a large shrub in the neighbourhood park.

"Stop, Mom!" Lauren said. She opened the door, flew across the green grass, and stooped. The boy was trying to coax the little dog out from under the bush, but the dog snarled at him each time.

He didn't snarl at Lauren, allowing her to pat his head. But he wouldn't budge. Lauren hurried back to car.

"Julius!" she said. "I need Julius."

Somehow, she and Julius managed to coax the little dog from under the bush. She brought him back to the car, trying to soothe him with soft whispers.

"You're okay now," she kept saying. "You're safe."

He looked pitiful. His fur was covered with burrs and small twigs, and he looked very, very tired.

Back at our home, Lauren fed and watered him, got most of the burrs out, bathed him. That same day, she took him to the vet then she and I went from door to door in the neighbourhood trying to find his owner.

Finally, one man gave us hope. We had stopped him just as he was reversing his car out of his driveway.

"That's Daisy!" he said. "She belongs to my neighbour."

"Daisy?" Lauren asked, turning the dog upside down.

"No, I guess that's not Daisy," the neighbour said. "Daisy is a girl dog."

Lauren continued searching, helped by Aaron, the young neighbour who had tried to coax the little dog out from under the bush. He and his father posted a notice on light-posts around the neighbourhood.

No one came forward.

Lauren called the humane society almost every day to find out if the owner had turned up.

Two more weeks passed.

Now, at my strong urging, she took him to the humane society to hand him over. The kind lady there explained, pleasantly but matter of factly, "He's old. His teeth are in terrible shape, and he's got warts on his body. No one will want to adopt a dog like this."

We knew the alternative. He would have to be put down.

Lauren hugged the little dog even more tightly.

I tried to persuade her that, in his shape, this little creature was better off dead than alive, but she wasn't buying it.

"You raised us children to look out for the vulnerable!" Her words were laced with disappointment and anger. "Well, this little dog is vulnerable, and I'm looking out for him."

It was one of those times when a parent is completely lost for a reply.

Meantime, a neighbour who had seen the poster telephoned our home. After hearing about the dog's medical troubles and Lauren's determination to help him, she and her neighbours raised two hundred dollars to help.

It was the same at Lauren's workplace. Her colleague Susan Antonacci, the editor-in-chief of *Canadian Living Magazine*, raised funds for most of the veterinary bills. That was a relief for Lauren, as she had been footing them on her own.

To make matters better – or worse – Julius had already developed a protective affection for Dawson, sleeping beside him, licking his fur occasionally, keeping an eye on his whereabouts.

He and Lauren had both bonded with the little one, but I wouldn't give up.

"You can't take care of another dog!" I kept telling Lauren. "And we won't!"

"I can! I will!" she replied.

And so she did.

Chapter Twenty-two

Home for Christmas

One December day two years earlier, Nikisha and Lauren came into my bedroom, where I was stuck in bed, and said they would decorate the house and dress the Christmas tree by themselves.

It pleased me to hear this.

"We're also going to replace the old ornaments, Mum," Nikisha said. "They're really dated and tattered."

"And ugly," Lauren added.

I laughed, but, as I told their father later, "The little wretches – those awful children of yours – sneaked into the basement, removed all of the ornaments from their boxes, and got rid of them! Without even asking me!"

"That does sound a bit high-handed." He didn't meet my eyes. "They should have at least asked your permission."

His voice seemed to lack conviction. "But I think they kept the really nice ones … and the others were kinda old and tattered."

So he hated them, too.

How could I have lived with these people so long and not known they hated my old ornaments?

Elder daughter even informed us we had been stringing

the Christmas tree lights incorrectly all these years. "You shouldn't hang them all over the ends of the branches," she said, adopting the tone of a Martha Stewart. "You need to wrap some of them around the tree trunk or hang them close to it so the tree will seem to be lit from within."

"Lit from within," I repeated with a groan.

I had to agree that the new lighting looked lovely. But it took me a good long time to tell them the new ornaments were nicer than the old ones.

~

Nikisha and Tim had settled into attending a church in downtown Toronto, but in the years after their wedding, they attended the Christmas Eve service with us at St. Thomas' Anglican. Then they returned to their own home and joined us at the farmhouse on the afternoon of Christmas Day. Extended family and close friends always joined us for Christmas Dinner.

That was the tradition. But this year, Nikisha and Tim would not be with us. Both had been repeatedly approached by recruiters for jobs in other cities and countries. Hamlin and I knew the day might come when we would lose them to greener pastures, but we consoled ourselves that they were comfortable in their jobs and in the narrow red-brick house he and I had once owned and they had unexpectedly bought back nearly twenty years later.

Then Tim was offered a better job – a promotion within his company – in Seattle, Washington. It was too good for him to pass up.

Their Toronto home sold quickly. Arrangements were made for their furniture and belongings to be shipped. Tim, Nikisha, and the cats, Simon and Jerome, would now be living far away from us.

Hamlin, Lauren, and I could feel their excitement at

starting a new phase of their lives. But the photos taken of our family at the airport showed reddened eyes and puffy eyelids.

When would we see them again? I still found long-distance travel to be immensely painful.

"Christmas will be quiet this year," one of us would say, while pretending we were not moping. For the most part, we nursed our sadness individually.

We decided to delay our traditional Christmas dinner with family and friends by a day. With the pain I was suffering, I needed to rest between the Christmas Eve festivities at church and the big dinner. Besides, all things considered, a quiet Christmas Day seemed to be in order this year.

~

We got up early on Christmas morning and had a light breakfast, followed by a hearty Jamaican brunch: ackee and codfish, Jamaica's national dish, along with bammies (plain white cassava cakes), biscuits, sliced avocados, and fruit juice and coffee.

After brunch, we eyed the Jamaican Christmas cake my sister Pat had made.

"Yummm," Lauren said.

"Yum, yum," I said.

"But we aren't touching it till after dinner!" Hamlin said.

"I hope you'll remember that, Dad!"

Then we sat on the living room floor, opened our presents, and joyfully thanked each other amidst squeals of surprise and delight.

But once in a while, one of us would ask, "I wonder if they're awake yet?"

There was no need to ask who "they" were.

Seattle was three hours behind southern Ontario.

"Is the inn where they're staying for Christmas in the Seattle area?" I asked.

"They said it was up in the mountains somewhere," Hamlin replied. "Pretty sure it isn't far from Seattle."

~

We phoned my uncles in London, England: Jack, Gerald, and Eddie. We always sent them loving Christmas cards, but made a habit of calling, too.

Then we settled down to watch our favourite Christmas movie, *The Holiday*. Hamlin sprawled on the sofa. Lauren created comfortable bedding for me on the floor then decided to join me there. I propped my legs on two cushions. Lauren's pet dogs Julius and Dawson made themselves at home beside us.

When we reached the part where one of the two lead characters sends her faithless lover packing, all three of us, once again, cheered her and jeered him.

"What a jerk!" I said, as if seeing the movie for the first time.

"A total jerk!" Lauren said.

Just then, the doorbell rang, sounding strangely out of place.

Yikes, I thought. My brother Michael probably forgot Christmas dinner was being held tomorrow.

Lauren got up first, and I followed more slowly.

Through the glass in the top half of the mudroom door, we glimpsed – no, it wasn't possible.

We looked again and both of us gasped.

There stood Nikisha and Tim, laughing.

"Open the door! We're freezing!" It was vintage Nikisha, pretending to be outraged that we had kept them waiting.

Lauren quickly opened the door and threw herself at them, tears flowing. I, who had stood still, seemingly paralyzed, did a half lunge forward, and hugged them, too.

"Dad, Dad!" Lauren hollered down the hallway. "Come now! They came! They came!"

Within seconds, we were all hugging and crying in the mudroom, forgetting to close the door.

"Going to a mountain inn for Christmas, eh?" Hamlin said after we had regained our senses.

"You had us completely fooled!" Lauren said.

Nikisha and Tim grinned, delighted that their ruse had worked.

"But where is everybody?" they asked.

"We changed the big dinner to tomorrow," I replied.

"Then I guess we got surprised, too," Tim said.

～

Our Christmas-on-Boxing-Day dinner was splendid. In addition to her usual Jamaican Christmas cake, Pat made a macaroni and cheese pie and a cassava pudding. Hamlin's mother made Jamaican-style fried fish and rice and peas. I made my usual sweet potato dish with apricots and raisins and baked the ham. Lauren made an enormous green salad.

Hamlin cooked the turkey and gravy.

We were all together. And that's what mattered most.

Chapter Twenty-three

In Bed with a Dead Poet

When you're ill for a long time – when pain racks your body, nightmares haunt your dreams, and you find it difficult to sleep and even breathe – you can slide into feeling sorry for yourself and forget what a blessed life you've had. That even to have lived this long was a blessing.

One day it occurred to me I'd already lived a lot longer than singer-poet Bob Marley, whose songs I could still hear in my head decades after his death: "Redemption Song." "No Woman No Cry."

Longer than Karen Carpenter, another singer-poet whose music I had loved in my teens and who, like Marley, died in her thirties. I went around my home crooning The Carpenters' songs. My favourites were "Close to You" and "We've Only Just Begun."

Longer than American civil rights leaders Martin Luther King and Malcolm X, who both died at age thirty-nine.

Longer than the reclusive nineteenth-century poet Emily Dickinson, known for her prolific output, including her famous poem that likens hope to a bird:

Hope is the thing with feathers

That perches in the soul,
And sings the tune without the words
And never stops at all ...

Longer, even, than my own grandfather, a brilliant wordsmith and inventor who never became world famous but whose legend lives on in our family. Like Dickinson, he was in his fifties when he died.

And way longer than John Keats, the English poet who wrote such marvellous lines as "Thou was not born for death, immortal bird!" from "Ode to a Nightingale" and, from "Endymion":

A thing of beauty is a joy forever.
Its loveliness increases; it will never
Pass into nothingness; but still will keep
A bower quiet for us, and a sleep
Full of sweet dreams, and health, and quiet breathing.

~

Some poets had privileged lives.

Not John Keats. His father died when the children were young. His mother remarried. Her new husband abused her, took the family's money then disappeared.

John later spent years caring for his brother Tom, who had tuberculosis, knowing it meant he would become infected, too.

John loved his neighbour, Frances, and she loved him back. But he couldn't marry her. He couldn't even touch her. He had contracted tuberculosis by then.

One autumn day in 1819, John took a walk near Winchester, England. He came home and wrote "Ode to Autumn," including the lines:

Season of mists and mellow fruitfulness,
Close bosom-friend of the maturing sun;

Conspiring with him how to load and bless
With fruit the vines that round the thatch-eves run ...

John died two years later, aged twenty-five, thinking himself a complete failure. He asked that no name be put on his tombstone, saying: "I have left no immortal works behind me, nothing to make my friends proud of my memory but I have loved the principle of beauty in all things, and if I had had time I would have made myself remembered."

"Ode to Autumn" became one of the best-loved poems in the English language, and John Keats became world famous – more than a century after he died.

How truly remarkable, I told myself as I read his poems in bed, to be so talented, to be able to see beauty in all things. And how truly awful, I thought, as I read his story, to die so young, believing you had accomplished nothing of worth.

His poems gave me a much needed boost that week. But for a little while, I also felt like weeping – for a man I'd never met.

Chapter Twenty-four

Angels

My staircase looked as tall as Mount Everest.

My back and leg were in terrible pain. But there was no alternative: I needed to fetch something upstairs in my office. I would have to climb the mountain on all fours.

Stair by stair, on hands and knees I went, a loud groan escaping my chest as if coming from someone else – a very old, very ill person. A disturbing sound.

At the top landing, I sat for a while, feeling miserable. But the effort required to make the trip upstairs to my office was worth it. An email came from Hamlin, who had left for work early that morning.

"Forgot to tell you," he wrote. "I heard a cardinal singing this morning. I looked out the kitchen door and saw a female ... the male must have been nearby."

I could almost see the beautiful red bird, perched on a tree branch. Could almost hear its distinctive whistle-song. Could almost believe spring had really arrived and winter was finally over.

~

It was late afternoon and daughter Lauren's little dog Dawson was visiting. He woke up and headed downstairs. It was time for his walk.

I followed him, picked him up, sat on the window seat in the kitchen, and held his squirming little body firmly on my lap then reached for his wool sweater. Before he could make a fuss, I located the appropriate openings in the garment and slipped his head and two front paws through them. Then I pulled the rest of the contraption over his body, still marvelling at the very idea that dogs had their own sweaters.

I opened the door of the mudroom, letting Dawson out ahead of me. The words "Bells of Vienna" were etched on the central column of the thick metal chimes on the verandah, and when the wind caressed them, you could understand why.

Angels on harps could do no better.

I slowly followed Dawson's paw-steps into the garden. Winter was not quite over. Snowflakes swirled around us in the breeze.

Dawson was so small, the low boxwood shrubs that circled the centre garden bed nearly obscured him. At one point I couldn't see him at all, though he was standing just a few feet away. Then I saw a blur of black-and-white sweater speeding around the boxwood circle.

We retraced our steps to the verandah, where I saw a small box leaning against the door, my name clearly written on it. Once we were back inside, I tore open the cardboard. There was a book inside, Elizabeth Gilbert's *The Signature of All Things*. I had been wanting to read it.

A short note accompanying the book read: "For Cynthia, who notices things 'close up' and understands in both visceral and transcendent ways the 'Signature of All Things' and can write so beautifully even when she hurts."

It was from Jacqui Denomme, who worked at the London Public Library. How did she know? I wondered. How did she know that, on a day like today, this gift would cheer me up no end?

I smiled. The angel at work again.

~

My sister Pat had asked me to find some information for her. I had. But now she was on the phone asking for the answer, and I couldn't remember what it was I'd found.

Too much pain, too little sleep, for days and nights on end. When I tried to speak, all that came out was a painful stutter. For just a moment, I almost burst into tears.

Pat recognized the warning signs. "Don't worry," she said. "We'll talk later. Just stop and rest now. Rest."

~

Sometimes the angel is a sound: the song of a cardinal on a winter day (or a note from a kind husband who hears it and tells me); the harmony played by the wind chimes on our verandah.

Sometimes the angel is a relative or friend. Nikisha and Tim, sending flowers, for no special reason. Long-time friend Kamala-Jean, calling me, out of the blue. Or Jacqui from London, Ontario, sending me that book.

Sometimes the angel is my sister, who knows me well enough to know when I'm in trouble.

And sometimes the angel is a scruffy-looking stranger. The young man who rushed to open a heavy door for me one afternoon as I left a store, a kind smile illuminating his face.

I imagine if the angel ever showed up as herself, she'd look like my mother, with soft brown skin and short, silver-grey hair, the very picture of serenity. In the meantime, she takes different forms and sounds and brings me joy when I least expect it.

"How do you manage to project positive thoughts on your blog when you're feeling so miserable?" my friend Pia asked me one day.

She often worked in Europe and Asia and read my blog regularly as one way of keeping in touch. Then, back in Canada, she paid me a sudden visit and found me struggling to get around.

"When I write my blog, I try to uplift my readers," I replied. "I focus on the blessings and joys of my life. Not sure what it does for them, but it sure makes me feel better."

At that, we both laughed and sipped our tea.

Of course, I should have also said, "Did I ever tell you about the angel?"

Chapter Twenty-five

The Mysterious Valentine Card

On Valentine's Day, 2014, I asked Hamlin: "Have you ever noticed your Valentine card?"

He became still, thoughtful, attentive. A man must be careful when it comes to birthdays, anniversaries, Valentine's Day, or what to say about his wife's new hairstyle.

"Of course I do," he said, after a short pause, wary of a trap. "But what about it?"

"Have you noticed how similar it is?"

"Similar?"

"Yes. Similar to last year's and the year's before."

"That can't be true. The same card?"

He regarded me with eyes narrowed, as if wondering whether the long stretch of ill health and lack of sleep was making me hallucinate. Finally he asked: "How did you do that?"

"Well, you always open the card, say: 'That's lovely, thank you.' Then you put it down on your bedside table and it gets covered up by magazines, books, and even letters. So I bide my time then rescue it and put it safely away in a drawer."

"You mean you save the card and give it to me a whole year later? In the same envelope?"

"Yes. And on Valentine's eve, as you sleep, I quietly place it on your bedside table, and when you get up you open it, and say, 'That's lovely, thank you.' There's such joy on your face that my heart smiles with pleasure. But the card gets covered up all over again by books, magazines, and other stuff. So I take the same steps all over again ... until the next Valentine's eve."

He was silent now.

Perplexed.

Befuddled.

Dumbfounded.

His face broke into a smile, then laughter. Hoots, whoops, eruptions of laughter. Followed by a kiss.

He didn't ask me why I did this. And I didn't tell him this was the year I had meant to go out and finally buy him a new card. But then my health had gone crazy, and I'd lost track of the weeks and Valentine's Day had sneaked up on me, so I resorted to my old tricks.

Late in the night, something woke me up.

A sniffle? No, a snuffle. No, a snort ... of laughter. From Hamlin.

I did my best to pretend I was asleep, but the giggle bubbled up then burst out of my body.

The next day, he handed me the card. "Here," he said, "you'll want to save this."

Chapter Twenty-six

Friends

From my journal, undated:

> We went to church after several weeks' absence.
> It was lovely to be there. To greet and be greeted
> so warmly by our friends. St. Thomas' is such
> an important part of our lives ... for the gospel,
> the rituals and our friendships. For that hour on
> Sunday morning, I feel as if I'm closer to goodness,
> closer to God, closer to those around me.

~

Hamlin and I know everyone at the early service at St.
Thomas'. When we miss a service, a concerned parishioner calls to make sure we're okay.

"Is this the church police calling?" I always tease the
caller, knowing full well by the voice whether it's Jane,
Muriel, Joanne, or Reverend Claire herself.

~

Jane, in her mid-seventies, with short reddish hair turning
grey, was one of the most active volunteers in our church.
She managed St. Thomas' archives – photos and other

records of our church's history going back to the late 1800s. She managed the "readers' list," making sure there were always two volunteers to read the Bible lessons each Sunday morning. And she was often "on chancel duty," meaning she helped the priest to serve communion.

Years before, when I had the very responsible role of church warden, I especially appreciated the contributions of Jane and other hardworking volunteers at the church.

And yet, friendship with Jane was not immediate. She didn't seem to smile much. She did her work quietly and did not seek out small talk. On the few occasions when she and I spoke, she answered frankly then returned immediately to what she was doing.

Jane was doing even more than I knew. A former teacher, she had a way with children and, in various ways, helped several church members who had young families.

Then came a Sunday morning several years after our family started attending. I made an offhand comment to her, and, unexpectedly, her blue eyes sparkled and her face crinkled into laughter. I had never seen her laugh like that, and, before I knew it, I was hooting, too. We were no longer grown women with very responsible church roles, but children sharing a belly laugh at something silly – and finding it the funniest thing in the world.

The thing is, once you've seen the laughing child in a person's face, it's hard to not like them. Gradually, Jane and I became friends.

Then came the car accident, our family's move from the village, and my mother's death … all these events took place within the same year. Hamlin and I were missing from church for months.

Over subsequent years, there would be many more absences. The long drive to and from church and sitting on a hard, narrow wooden pew amounted to nearly three hours of physical torture. On many Sundays, it was simply too much.

When we did go to church I worked hard to maintain a cheerful facade. I distracted those who mentioned my limp with a deliberately uplifting counter-question: "And how are *you* doing today?" I would linger just long enough to hear the reply then move on.

I saw the hurt in Jane's eyes the first time she realized that my injuries were far more extensive than met the eye. I had missed church and missed our friends there and wanted desperately to return. But Hamlin and I both knew this was a bad day: I was bleary-eyed and stuttering, and the pain had not abated. Our plan was to do what we usually did on such days: leave right after the service.

Jane approached to ask me a question as we headed to the door. I stuttered and stared at her blankly. Panicked by the slip, I was just about to shut down the conversation – closing her out the way I'd done to so many others.

Surprise, then a dawning realization, showed on her face.

I wanted to bolt. I looked around for Hamlin to intervene or help me escape, but he was talking to someone else. I heard Jane sigh and, looking back, saw her shoulders slump.

Jane had unexpectedly pierced my armour of silence, but she also realized I was about to shut down.

"I'll c-c-call you," I whispered. "I'll … explain."

I put off the phone call until I couldn't put it off any longer.

Haltingly, I described to Jane the severity of the pain that hounded me day and night; my fear that even mentioning the accident and its impact would bring on yet another PTSD-induced attack, which would trigger yet another bout of depression. In shame, I confessed that

I was sure I was developing Alzheimer's disease. How else to explain my frequent inability to remember, think, or speak?

"Thank you for telling me, Cynthia," she said. "I'm so sorry for all you're going through. But you know, you shouldn't be worried about sharing this with our church community. That's what we're there for."

Instead of agreeing, I swore Jane to silence.

~

Jane is a good keeper of confidences. She told no one. But her behaviour toward me changed. She telephoned often, gently inquiring about my health but also sensing when talking was too difficult. She was the only person from our church whose phone call I took on days when my speech and mind had gone crazy.

~

When you have been ill for a long time, when you are no longer out and about where people can see you, share personal updates, and regularly renew the ties of friendship, it's easy to be forgotten.

Jane remembered me, and she showed it in several ways. Every other week or so, she sent me a greeting card, sometimes with an encouraging note included.

~

Returning to church one Sunday morning after another prolonged absence, I found that a cushion had already been placed on the seat where I usually sat, in the back pew of our small chapel. Soon Jane also brought a short footstool from home so I could prop up my foot and leg during the service. Her way of saying, "I can't help you with the other issues, Cynthia, but I can help make you physically comfortable."

She even had a backup. On Sundays when she missed church, Joanne put my cushion and footstool in place.

During the coffee hour, Jane always sat right next to me. Without ever mentioning what she had learned about my injuries, she was doing her best to protect me.

My name had occasionally been on the prayer list in the first year after the accident and then it disappeared. Jane now made sure that it stayed there, adding Hamlin's name as well.

"Hamlin needs prayers, too," she said. "He's the one taking care of you."

Then came an extremely rough patch – I was so beleaguered by pain, sleeplessness, and PTSD attacks that I'd fallen into a profound depression. I missed church several times in a row, and refused to answer the phone when anyone called.

Jane called several times. I didn't return her call.

Finally, Hamlin put his foot down. "Cynthia, you need to call Jane! Now!"

~

And then, one day, I was finally strong enough, considerate enough, to realize something important. That making Jane part of the small circle of people who knew the secret had put a heavy burden on her shoulders.

Consumed by the impact of my injuries on my family and very close friends, I had failed to consider loved ones outside that tight circle. Worse, the hyper-vigilance I adopted to stave off anxiety attacks and recognize the signs of worsening pain required a level of self-monitoring that left little time for me to think of others.

But now I had to think of someone else. After years of painful conversations, it was time to remove some of the burden from Jane's shoulders.

Out of nowhere came the idea that I needed to make Jane laugh. Yes, I would inquire more about her life and listen more attentively to her replies. But when she asked about my health, I would give her a humorous description of what I was going through. I would do this every time we spoke.

Later, I would have to confront a thing that scared me: opening up to my other friends. But right now, I simply needed to make Jane laugh.

～

The stuttering, the inability to remember or think clearly, and the crushing shame of what I had become had pushed me farther and farther away from most of my friends. A few, realizing that I was in trouble, called repeatedly, often settling for a chat with Hamlin instead.

I had been apprehensive about releasing the memoir, but that gave way to relief; the book described some of the challenges I still didn't trust myself to talk about, even with close friends. I figured the book would help them understand.

Long-time friend Eva was among the first to respond. "I should have known something was terribly wrong," she said. "You just disappeared."

Not long after, she called again, inviting Hamlin and me to visit her home along with a small group of mutual friends and asked if I would read a few short excerpts from the book.

Sitting in Eva's cosy living room, I started tentatively then slowly gathered strength as I looked around at the caring faces: Kamala-Jean, Erica, Neil, Sandra, Karen, Lorna, and several others. Some stood nearby; some sat closely together. All radiated support.

～

The emails and phone calls from many friends and acquaintances echoed Eva's remark, expressing shock and remorse.

"But how could you have known?" I asked, over and over. "Please don't blame yourself."

I also didn't have a monopoly on hardship. Some friends, I discovered, had been coping with their own disasters. From thousands of kilometres away came a letter from a cherished friend and former colleague:

> *I was very touched ... but somewhat shamed as well, and also very sad, to realize that I had not fully grasped the depths of what you had gone through, and was of such little support, because I was so very lost in my own traumas, not fully registering until today that it was at the very same time. So there were the two of us, on opposite sides of the country, withdrawing and withering from life, without the means to reach out, either one to the other ... Who knows if we might have helped save each other from our darkest selves, if we had not been feeling too sick to let it be known.*
>
> *In any case, we are where we are today, in and out of different hells and back. And you, my friend, have turned your losses into a gift of beauty and poetry and hope for your growing number of readers! How great is that! It was wonderful to hear my old friend surfacing and blossoming, and ... as the old you has always done ... giving so freely to those around you. So thank you for fighting your good fight. Thank you to Hamlin for loving you back to life. Thank you for writing your story. Thank you for sharing it with us through your book.*

"Ah, my friend," I wrote back:

> *We have gone through such hell over these years.*

What a time it's been. But this, too, is life, and part of "growing up."

I no longer think anyone I know has a charmed life. As my mother used to say, "Everybody is dealing with something." And in my case, talking about it was so rough, I mostly went into a hole and "withdrew and withered," as you say.

But I think we should always remember that no matter what is happening, friendship like ours is always there, even when we're out of touch.

~

"The problem with keeping hardships to oneself," I later wrote in my journal, "is that it cheats those who love us from helping. You'd think that would be pretty obvious. So why did it take me years to figure it out?"

My mother's voice softly replied: "Ah m'dear. Life is a series of lessons. We live and learn."

Chapter Twenty-seven

Lent and Borrowed

Lent takes place each year in the weeks before Easter. Depending on the timing of Easter, it starts in February or early March.

"What are you giving up for Lent?" is a common question, usually asked around Ash Wednesday, the day that signals the beginning of this period. It's a time of reflection and contemplation for Christians, and, for many, a time of fasting and other forms of sacrifice.

"I'm giving up guilt and shame," I told Hamlin. I knew, of course, that it would take a while to give up those vices, and added, "Okay, I'll think of something more achievable during Lent."

But – my saner self pointed out – what was the point?

I'd no sooner make the commitment than I'd forget it. Then I'd feel like a failure and end up with guilt and shame yet again.

I settled on what I sometimes ended up doing during this time: reading a book with a spiritually challenging theme.

One year, I became engrossed in a thin book by W. Phillip Keller, its sole subject being the twenty-third psalm, the ancient and much-loved affirmation from the

Bible that begins: "The Lord is my shepherd, I shall not want."

How could anyone write a whole book about a short psalm? And why? My disbelief was soon replaced with intrigue. A shepherd himself, Kerr writes about the character of a good shepherd and the ways of sheep. He takes us back to the time this psalm was written and explains what some of the pastoral terms mean in that context.

I found myself reflecting on what it was like to have such complete trust in God. It wasn't something I possessed, or even fully understood.

My mother had, and her trust in God had given her a serenity that I craved. She truly believed God's mercy and goodness were with her every day of her life.

During Lent, my quest for a deeper faith in God became stronger. I prayed – not just a hurried bedtime prayer but several talks with God each day.

And when I read a book, I made notes, reminders of renewed commitment to learning. Tools for developing a more spiritually fulfilling and balanced life.

Of course, that was always more easily said than done. Especially so during that brutal winter.

~

The Book of Common Prayer – fondly called the BCP by many Anglicans – is small, fat, and covered with burgundy cloth. It contains many prayers, the Book of Psalms, and other passages from the Old Testament. It also includes a few sentences that make me cringe, even fume.

I learned to hurry past the Old Testament belief that a loving God would hold a person responsible for the sins of previous generations.

But only after complaining to our priest.

"I mean, really," I told Reverend Claire as I stood in the queue waiting to shake her hand after the service.

"This is horrible. I simply do not accept the idea of such a vengeful God."

Unruffled, Reverend Claire said something like "this calls for a longer conversation," which we both knew was unlikely to happen. It wasn't the first thing I'd questioned in the Bible or the BCP, and it wouldn't be the last. But sometimes, she knew, I just needed to vent.

I could almost hear my mother whispering: "In life, sometimes you just have to take the bad with the good and carry on."

Truth is that, despite some quibbles and downright disagreements between the BCP and me, I had grown to love the little book, especially its prayers. The language is beautiful in many parts, the sentiments radiant with hope and trust.

There are prayers for a variety of human seasons and situations: for a good harvest, for those voyaging on the high seas, for births and marriages, for the dying.

There are prayers for support "until the shadows lengthen and the evening comes, the busy world is hushed, the fever of life is over, and our work is done."

There are prayers for teachers, for "the spirit of wisdom and grace, that they may lead their pupils to reverence truth, desire goodness and rejoice in beauty."

There's even a prayer for anxious souls. "Regard with thy tender compassion those in anxiety and distress; bear their sorrow and their cares ..."

I found the prayers so comforting that – completely disobeying the famous commandment against stealing – I "borrowed" a copy from church one Sunday and kept it at home throughout the winter.

"How can you steal a book from a church?" Hamlin immediately asked when he spied me reading the BCP in bed and I told him what I had done.

"Under the circumstances," I said, smiling, "I figured that God would approve."

God might have approved, but Hamlin didn't. His reaction reminded me of the only other time I had taken a book – two, actually, those ones from a convent of Anglican nuns. I hadn't realized that I had put them in my suitcase during a weekend retreat there. Coming across them at home, I had taken my time to read them before returning them – a whole year later.

"I only steal from holy places," I told Hamlin this time, smiling even more mischievously. "And, furthermore," I added when he still didn't answer, "the nuns were glad I read the books. They were both about deepening one's faith."

Hamlin was not amused.

"I later went back and told Rev. Claire that I had removed the copy of the BCP, you know," I said.

"What did she say?"

"That I was welcome to keep it for as long as I needed. And that she had borrowed a few books from churches, too."

"Borrowed, Cynthia. Not stolen." Hamlin wasn't letting me off the hook.

I shrugged. Strangely enough, I felt no guilt.

That, in itself, was an accomplishment ... if only in my book.

～

Winter took its toll that year. What I remember most were all the days I was stuck in bed. Worn out and afraid of falling, I rarely went outside.

Too ill to attend church in months now, I used the small burgundy book to "follow" the order of the 8:30 service from home – joyfully at times, conscience-stricken at others. Not over the "stolen" book but the much bigger things that haunted me.

One Sunday morning my eye caught the words, "We have left undone those things which we ought to have done. And we have done those things which we ought not to have done."

"You got that right," I thought. So much I hadn't done. So much I couldn't do.

This time, it was myself that I had ignored. This last relapse was a result of forgetting my promise to my doctors and therapist. I was so excited to be an author, so flattered by all the letters from readers and all the book readings, that I hadn't paced myself. Hadn't done all my daily exercises. Hadn't rested enough. Hadn't even gone to physiotherapy. Instead, I was swallowing too many painkillers each day.

Worst of all, I could feel myself doing the thing I had promised myself I would not allow: sinking into depression. The old despair was coming back, bringing with it that dreaded streak of guilt and anger at myself.

Sarah, my therapist, had recently moved to Vancouver. We had agreed to continue our weekly meetings by Skype, but I could never remember to do it. That should have been a sign I was falling down the mountain, but I think I already knew that, and didn't have the energy to care.

Chapter Twenty-eight

A Job That Pays

"Lying in bed," G.K. Chesterton wrote, "would be an altogether perfect and supreme experience if only one had a coloured pencil long enough to draw on the ceiling."

I made do with the blog my daughter set up for me and which I hadn't visited much until some months earlier. Notes in my journal became updates for the blog. The blog gave me something to do, but it did not bring in any money. And although book sales had been respectable, almost everything it earned went to paying off a loan I had incurred for editing services. With the condition I had been in during the rewriting and completion phases of the book, I had needed to pay not just one editor but three.

Worried, yet again, about Hamlin, I wished there was something I could do to lessen the load he carried as the sole breadwinner.

I rarely spent money these days. You can't spend what you don't have, I told myself.

Strangely, I no longer felt sad about not being able to shop for new clothes. It was one of the many things I had grown to accept. The one thing that still made me cringe, however, was asking my husband for money for things like toiletries. He never complained, but I never got used to this loss of independence.

I had become dependent on him in many ways, but this ongoing financial dependence was hard to bear.

～

The great Scottish teacher Oswald Chambers famously declared that one can't stay on the mountaintop all the time. It's "down in the valley" where we are made.

Maybe so, I thought more than once that winter. But I'm sick of the valley.

～

The Idea seized my mind just as my good man walked into the room. In truth, I was probably hallucinating. Over several months, I'd consumed a pharmacopia of drugs for pain and other ailments then taken more drugs to counteract the side-effects.

"I have an idea," I said.

"Oh, boy! Let's hear it."

"I'm going to look for a job a person can do lying on her back."

He laughed.

"No, not that one."

He was still laughing.

"Let's be real," I said. "I've spent a lot of time in bed. So I need to find a job I can do in bed!"

"You write in bed ..."

"Writing doesn't pay much. I need a job that pays!"

"Okay. So how do you plan to find such a job?"

Time to bring out the big guns, I thought.

"I'm going to place an ad somewhere. It will say, WANTED: A Job That Can Be Done Lying Down."

He squinted. Raised his eyebrows. Let them fall into place again. And sighed.

"Knowing you, you just might do that. But have you considered the replies you'd get?"

Even under the influence of drugs, I got the picture.

"Okay – forget the ad. But seriously: apart from writing, there must be jobs a person can do lying down. Jobs I'd be good at ...?"

But we still couldn't think of any.

"Unless ..." a friend said later that day.

"Unless what?"

"Well, there are those ads on TV – for phone sex. That must be a job you can do from your bed."

"Oh no!" I replied. "Kill me now!"

Chapter Twenty-nine

No More Calls from Paddy

Although our neighbours Paddy and Jacqui lived just down the street, I had not seen them in recent weeks. They had left to visit their daughter in the American southwest, and though they called to tell us they had returned safely, I could not visit.

In addition to the pain, I had a bad flu and cold, with a cough that wouldn't stop.

In a matter of weeks, Paddy was hospitalized. Diagnosed with a disease from which few people recover: pancreatic cancer.

I still couldn't visit. The flu and cough had become bronchitis and a sinus infection. Before that was over, I got a stomach virus.

Paddy was brought home in March. Although Jacqui was careful about how she described his condition, a mutual friend told us he had a short time left.

I called Jacqui as often as I could without being a bother. Finally, one Saturday a few weeks later, she asked if I could come over to stay with Paddy while she went on an errand.

This time I was past the contagious stage and happy I could help.

"He's in bed, mostly resting," Jacqui told me when I arrived. "There's a dish of fruit on the dresser, and there's a glass of water. Try to get him to eat and drink some."

I followed her up the stairs to the big bed in the master bedroom. Paddy was a short, slender man. Lying there, sheet drawn up to his neck, he looked even smaller.

"Cynthia's here, Paddy," Jacqui said.

Paddy smiled weakly. "Cynthia!" he said in a hoarse whisper.

"I'm here, darling Paddy."

~

How could our family not love this man? He and Jacqui had looked out for us from the day we moved in to the farmhouse. They had shown up with a basket of fruit drinks and Jamaican-style fish fritters.

Being of Chinese ancestry, Paddy believed in the effectiveness of Asian remedies.

"A friend told me about an ointment for pain," he said one day. "Want me to pick some up at the Chinese store and bring it for you? Don't worry – you can pay me later."

Then there was his relationship with Kinu, the enormous Akita who thought he was small. Paddy would come through the kitchen door, and Kinu would rush to greet him, almost knocking him over.

What a picture the two of them made. Standing on his hind legs, Kinu was a tower of gold fur, several inches taller than Paddy. It always took Kinu a minute or so to return to all fours, so excited was he to see him.

"My friend! My friend!" Paddy would say after a balancing act to keep himself from falling. "How are you today?"

And then Kinu would get even more excited, and Paddy would have to hug Kinu close to his body to keep them both steady. Kinu's gladness had a way of showing in every fibre of his being as he reached his big hairy dark brown head close to kiss Paddy's face.

When Kinu got old and infirm and died, Paddy sent us a note of condolence, knowing we had lost a member of our family, and he had lost a friend.

Whenever he and Jacqui dropped in, he paused in the mudroom, remembering Kinu. You would think he would have been relieved that he was no longer being knocked off his feet.

"I miss my friend," he would say.

Paddy visited our home often. Knowing I was often housebound, he always called before he and Jacqui left home to do their weekly grocery shopping. Jacqui had already scoped out the specials at one or more supermarkets.

"No Frills has a great price on pomegranate juice," Paddy would say. "Want me to pick some up for you?"

In the summer, they sought out the best prices on mangoes and always dropped some off on their way home.

I thanked my lucky stars for such good neighbours.

~

Phil and Marje, mutual friends, were there at the house that Saturday, as were two others. Chairs for visitors had been positioned at one end of the large room facing the bed, and we took turns sitting there.

Paddy loved a joke, and he liked being teased. So we took turns teasing him between the times when he rested. It was wonderful to see him smile.

Mostly, I stayed by Paddy's bed. Every so often, I hugged him, told him I loved him, and offered him some fruit. He took only one or two pieces of diced papaya each time.

"Fix the pillows," he whispered. "I need to sit up." Phil

and Marje rearranged the pillows while I hugged Paddy to prevent him from falling back.

I had hugged him on many occasions, but never had he felt so frail. So fragile.

Paddy had a surprising request: Would I help steady him so he could exercise his feet and legs? The therapist had advised him to move them regularly to help his blood circulation.

"Of course," I said.

In the hours while I visited, Paddy made this request twice. Each time, Phil and I would help raise him up from the pillows supporting his back, and help him move his body toward the window. Near the ground under the windowsill was a ledge, which Paddy used as a lever for his exercises.

Where did I get the strength? Well, I figured if a dying man – a frail, fragile man – could get up from his bed and do his exercises, ignoring my own pain was the least I could do.

～

They say people who are dying make a supreme effort to wait until the last of their loved ones arrive.

Paddy's sister arrived from Britain late that evening.

The next day, we got a call that Paddy was gone. He had died early that morning.

～

It was two weeks after the funeral, but that there would be no more phone calls from Paddy inquiring about my health, telling me about supermarket specials, no more Paddy buying us mangoes or just dropping in for a chat … it was hard to believe.

Paddy had always been the first person we called when something broke down. He always knew "just the guy" to repair a leaky roof or a kitchen appliance or to update our electrical panel.

"If we miss him so much, can you imagine poor Jacqui?" I asked Hamlin.

She was, of course, grieving, but she was not the kind to talk about it. Instead, she kept herself busy sorting Paddy's clothes and shoes and giving them to friends.

Hamlin received an assortment of small items, including a baseball cap and a key chain. Occasionally Jacqui also called him when a task required greater strength than she possessed. We made a point of calling her every few days to see what we could do to help. But I privately wondered what would happen to our relationship with her. After all, Paddy had almost always been the one to call.

One afternoon, Jacqui phoned. "Are you going to be there in a few minutes? I'm coming for a visit."

I bustled around the kitchen and plugged in the kettle to make tea.

When Jacqui arrived, I took her coat and we hugged, holding on to each other longer than normal.

We sat at the harvest table to have our tea. It was the same table that just last October was laden with produce from the garden – including the lone Jamaican pumpkin that grew from a seedling Paddy and Jacqui had given us that spring.

She had been going through Paddy's belongings, Jacqui said. Deciding what to give away and identifying matters that needed her immediate attention. Then she opened Paddy's briefcase, and her eyes fell on an envelope in his handwriting addressed, "To My Wife."

"I want you to read it," Jacqui said, sliding the long white envelope across the harvest table toward me. She had torn it open at one end.

I got goosebumps as I read, aloud:

My dearest Jacqui.

So faithful and true!

Without you, I would have had nothing. It was due to your sacrifices that we survived. You gave so much and demanded so little. Thank you for being so much to me over the years ...

If you are reading this, it means that I've passed on. Don't be sad. Our life together was good! Although I won't be here in body, I will always be at your side in spirit.

Goodbye, my love!

I dared not look at Jacqui's face. Partly because I knew I would cry and partly because I feared she would. Instead, I got up from my chair and hugged her again.

"That must have been a huge surprise," I said at last. "Did you have any idea he'd written this letter?"

"None at all."

But then Jacqui told me what surprised her most: the letter was dated August 9, 1999. Paddy had written it nearly fifteen years earlier. He'd placed it in his briefcase with other important papers, where he knew Jacqui would find it if he died before she did.

～

We hurt when we lose someone we love. The greater the love, the deeper the hurt. But given a choice, who wouldn't choose love? And who wouldn't choose great love?

Jacqui was experiencing great pain.

After she left, I went upstairs to my office, grabbed a sheet of paper and a pen, and wrote a letter. I put it in a long white envelope, placing it on the top shelf behind my desk.

It was addressed "To My Dear Family."

Chapter Thirty

Lorna's Prayer

Lorna was my hairdresser.

Born in Jamaica, she had lived in Canada for most of her life. I never asked her age. With her smooth dark brown skin and a face that was quick to laugh, she could have been in her thirties, but one of her children was in her early twenties, so I figured Lorna was somewhere in her forties.

She put most of her energy into parenting them on her own after her marriage broke up. One of the reasons she moved her business from the big, fancy salon in a nearby plaza to her basement was to be home when her children got back from school each day.

Over the years, Lorna gradually decorated the large basement space, painting the walls a sunshine yellow with gleaming white trim, the wooden floors a medium brown shade, setting up a seating area for clients at one end of the room with plump green sofas, a TV, a stereo, and a magazine stand. Once in a while, someone would turn on the TV.

One afternoon, when a TV newsreader announced yet another story of a black teenager slain in Toronto, Lorna declared, "You see? That's why I'm so strict with my children. I don't ever want them to get into trouble. They think I'm too strict, but I have to be strict!"

Her clients nodded in agreement.

We had seen her interactions with her daughter and son: firm yet loving. We had watched the children grow up, start university and college, become young adults. We had rejoiced with Lorna over their successes. And when she remarried, we rejoiced over that, too.

Lorna sometimes reminded me of my own mother. That warm, welcoming presence. The way she loved to laugh and enjoyed a good joke.

～

My mother was a dressmaker who worked hard to raise and support her family.

Our father had been part of the migration of Jamaican men to jobs in the mother country, England, in the 1950s. He went to London to earn enough money to build a house big enough to accommodate his family of seven.

I remembered the women who came to our house to get their dresses sewn. The way my mother listened to them, commiserated with them, comforted them.

～

Lorna saw me on so many bad days that she knew when to ask me questions and when to just let me be.

If my back or leg ached ferociously, I had to get up, walk around, lie down, or lean against a wall to do some exercises.

If Lorna was washing my hair over the hairdresser's sink and I asked to get up right away, she acted as if this happened every day in her salon. She quickly threw a towel over my head to prevent my clothes and her floor from getting wet. Then she waited.

If tears rolled down my cheeks while she blow-dried my hair, no problem: she waited for me to get through that, too.

~

One morning when I arrived, Lorna said she would be in the salon soon. I asked to use the powder room before heading down.

A few minutes later, I was heading slowly down the hallway toward the basement stairs, when I heard a voice coming from the kitchen.

I glanced quickly through the doorway and saw Lorna seated at her kitchen table. Head bowed, she was talking on the speakerphone. A woman's voice answered. They were praying, each taking her turn.

I had arrived too early for my appointment and had interrupted a sacred moment.

I stood stock-still on the rug in the hallway, not knowing whether to keep walking or stay put. It was like that moment when the national anthem starts playing at a public dinner, or when a voice announces the start of that minute of silence on Remembrance Day.

Lorna's voice was raised, her English perfect. It seemed to belong to a completely different Lorna. She often spoke to me in a mix of Jamaican patois and English. But there was no patois this morning. And although she was praying to God, requesting his favour, her voice was stronger and more powerful than I'd ever heard it.

The only place I'd ever seen such a naked expression of faith was in the little village church my mother and grandmother had attended in Jamaica.

At home, my mother prayed daily, morning and evening (and, for all I know, at points in between). She always prayed on her knees. These were private prayers, and I had never dreamed of interrupting or eavesdropping.

I did not want to eavesdrop now, either.

Voice raised, Lorna thanked God for his many blessings. Her voice caught as she asked – no, beseeched – God to bless her children and her marriage.

Surely this is a private prayer, I thought. One I should not hear. I started to raise my foot to walk to the stairway to the basement, slowly, gently, so as not to disturb Lorna with the sound of my shoes and the clack of my cane on her floor.

"And God, I pray for every client that comes through my door. Bless them, God, and help them to be in a better condition than when they walked in."

I put my foot back down.

"God, you see my client, where she stands. Father, you know the pain and suffering that she has gone through over these years. You know even better than the rest of us. I pray that you will look upon her, dear God. I pray that you will strengthen her from the crown of her head to the soles of her feet.

"Please, God."

There was no mistaking the depth of feeling behind her entreaty to God. Or the fact that she was now crying. I'd never seen her cry before.

The moment was as potent as the time I watched elders in my mother's church form a circle around a young man, anoint his head with sacred oil, and pray fervently for his healing. Back then I was so moved I tried even to breathe more quietly. But back then I was outside the circle, watching and listening. Now I was inside the circle – Lorna's circle – and the prayer was for me.

The "amen" came at last. The moment passed. The ritual was over.

Lorna looked up at me and smiled, the sunshine breaking through the rain of her tears. She got up, grabbed a tissue, and wiped her eyes and face.

"Thank you, Lorna," I said.

I made my way down the hallway and down the stairs, murmuring, "Thank you, Lorna. Thank you, God."

Chapter Thirty-one

Spring Fever

It was May 2014. Time for my regular visit to my specialist. By now, so much had taken place that I had completely forgotten the potential loss of my driver's licence.

It's not as if I was driving that much, anyway.

Dr. Helen was not pleased with my progress. No big surprise, that. I was struggling to stay upright each day, the pain was intense, and my stuttering had returned, big time. The side effects of a new medication I was trying were so bad I had to get yet another prescription to counteract some of them.

The doctor stared at me and shook her head. I knew what she was thinking: with all these challenges, why did I keep pushing myself so hard?

"You've relapsed, again," she observed flatly.

"Guilty," I replied. "Sorry."

"Do not feel guilty," she said. "It was an awful winter. All my patients with complex injuries had a very tough time."

But she also issued a warning: "Your immune system is also weak. Be very careful this spring, Cynthia."

She calmly put me under house arrest: No book

readings, no book club visits. Stay home. Focus on your recovery.

I listened. I promised. The problem was that I loved spring. And every spring, I went a little crazy.

~

The first robin sang on the nest she had been building in the shrub just below our bedroom window:

Cheerily, cheeriup, cheerio, cheeriup.
Cheerily, cheeriup, cheerio, cheeriup.

It was early morning, but it was such a welcome sound that I threw back the covers on my side of the bed and got up smiling, happy to greet the day.

"Spring is here at last!" I told Hamlin. "Listen to the robin sing! Isn't it the loveliest sound?"

Hamlin growled something like "Uuuuurgh ..." (it may have been stronger) and pulled a pillow over his head.

~

If there's one time of year when a mostly sane person is totally justified in talking to flowers, it's early spring, right after a long and difficult winter.

On the newest arbour – the one Hamlin built for me over the side gate – the clematis was always the first vine to bloom. Against the white lattice of the arbour, its fuchsia-pink flowers nodded a happy greeting to all who passed by.

"Good morning, clematis," I answered. "And how are you this fine morning?"

It would bloom again in late summer, just after its companion clematis on the arbour had given us a lengthy show of blue-pink flowers.

To the left of that arbour, sprawled across the sturdy white picket fence, was the wisteria vine that bloomed twice and decided to quit. We had tried everything. More water. Less water. More fertilizer. Less fertilizer. Once, on the advice of a very experienced gardener, Hamlin even cut into a root to shock the vine.

When all that failed, as long as there was no one around to hear, we descended to begging, bribes, insults, and, finally, ominous threats of uprooting and throwing it on the compost heap.

Nothing we said, of course, made any difference.

It was now a mature twenty-three-year-old. And still, each year I hoped for blooms and fooled myself into thinking the unfurled leaves in early spring were really blossoms just waiting to bloom.

I had even taken to writing silly poems about this plant:

Wisteria, oh Wisteria
You drive me to hysteria ...

Not exactly William Wordsworth.

I imagined my tombstone bearing the words: *She succumbed to grief over her bloomless wisteria and hapless poetry ...*

But it was spring again. A time of hope. Hope that the long winter was truly past, and that it would be a good spring. Hope that our bodies would recover and our souls would be regenerated, reborn, and renewed, along with our gardens.

And even hope for our recalcitrant wisteria.

~

Our quiet neighbourhood came to life with the spring.

Lawns were fertilized. Chairs – and people to sit on them – suddenly reappeared on verandahs. People raked lawns. Pots of pansies were placed on the sides of front steps. The pansies' cheery little faces, in yellow, blue, and sometimes both yellow and blue together, seemed to smile at everyone who passed by.

Neighbours greeted each other, some for the first time since early winter, back when everyone migrated indoors and closed doors and windows against the cold. Conversations across our garden fence were almost entirely about the weather and gardens.

"Thank God the winter is over! Can you believe how harsh it was?"

"Yes, and there's still time for a killer frost ..."

"How's your lawn doing?"

"Some patches where the moles did their damage. But they eat grubs, so let's not complain too much."

"But the rabbits! So many rabbits! I'll have to put a fence around my back garden this spring!"

"Have you tried hot peppers?"

On and on it went, in our neighbourhood of gardeners. It was music to my ears. Much like the song of the robins.

~

Every morning and every evening, my husband worked in the garden. He worked hard. And I watched, feeling entirely useless.

The following day was Saturday – a prime gardening day – and he started early. After a couple hours, he left on an errand.

I took a deep swig of fresh air and warm sunshine and could feel them egging me on. I got up to stride through the garden. I did so at least five times a day.

At least, that's how I saw it: striding. My mischievous husband, however, had dubbed it "strimping" – a compromise between what I thought and what he clearly saw: a woman limping through the garden.

Strimping? I was not amused.

~

Months before, I had written myself a cautionary note. Written it in my journal:

Watch out for the good days.
You already know what to expect from the bad days. They sap your energy, wear you out, make you scream in pain.
But the good days? These are dangerous times, Cynthia. You feel energetic enough – and idiotic enough – to do something helpful. You think you're helping. That you simply must help. Don't be stupid.

~

Forget-me-nots are short, with flowers that are tiny. But, massed together in a garden bed, they look like clouds of blue radiating from the ground. They are prolific self-seeders. Seeds somehow find a way to grow even in a thick lawn. They are like truant children, determined to run away from home.

And as I stared at the lawn near the centre garden bed, I could see that several of them had done exactly that. Run away from the circular garden bed. Run right through the boxwood hedge. Run into the grass.

I knew the wandering forget-me-nots annoyed Hamlin, and I knew they were easy to pull up or dig out with a trowel. And so I thought I'd help. It was a small thing. And a good thing.

"I can do this," I told myself.

I fetched the trowel, crouched over the lawn, and started digging, feeling immensely useful. When my back and leg pain intensified, I lay on my front, face just above the grass. Dust particles from the soil floated into my nose and I sneezed. Then I spied a few dandelions nearby. I crouched over them, trowel engaged, cane nearby.

"Stop!" said my wiser self.

I listened. And I meant to. In just a few seconds.

But then, my sense of time did not kick in. It rarely did.

When I got up, the pain almost knocked me out. I staggered. Stumbled. Jabbed my cane on the ground to gain purchase.

"Cynthia! Cynthia!" came the panicked shout.

I had not heard my husband return.

~

I ask you, which is worse? To watch your partner struggle to do the gardening duties that you loved doing on top of everything else on his plate? Or to risk even worse pain – and his distress – by doing a few small gardening things to help?

Some days, I was almost used to the pain. It was with me all the bloody time. But the guilt? I never got used to watching him do all the gardening. It drove me nuts.

Hamlin shook his head, frustrated and angry. "Why do you do this? You know better!"

So I started obeying the doctor. Again. Vowed to spare my husband further distress. Again. Tried to cope with my guilt. Again. All stuff that requires a person to be not just smart, but wise.

But nobody ever accused you of being wise, I said to myself. And returned to strimping.

Chapter Thirty-two

How Hard Could It Be?

Anne Day is a remarkable woman who seems endlessly wise, resourceful, trustworthy.

You instinctively want to follow her.

And when she founded Company of Women, based in the lovely Canadian city of Oakville where she lived, a lot of people did.

Anne and the Company of Women had done much to inspire and empower women, particularly those who ran their own businesses. In the month of June 2014, the organization held its annual conference west of Toronto. The conference was titled Journey 2 Success.

The morning opened with a dynamic keynote speaker. Here was a woman whose husband left her broke and hiding from bill collectors but who went on to become a successful businesswoman, featured on the Oprah show.

She was dishing out empowerment to her audience and everyone lapped it up like people finding water in a desert.

Next, three women were invited to the stage, myself included. And that's when I realized the intimate little panel discussion I had envisioned nearly a year ago was meant to be for everyone attending the conference. I hadn't done anything like this in years.

Book readings to small groups, yes. But this kind of thing? No way. They terrified me.

So what was I doing here?

~

Nearly a year earlier, Anne Day read my book and wrote a powerful review of it in the newspaper she publishes.

Some weeks later, an invitation followed. Would I take part in a panel discussion at the Company of Women conference next year?

I hesitated.

First, I talked to my family, who asked if I felt able to handle it then cautiously encouraged me to give it a try.

Sure, I emailed Anne, feeling bolder now.

I can handle talking with a few women, I thought. I know I can.

The Very Sane Voice at the back of my head kept asking: "Are you sure you can do this? What would your doctors and therapist say?"

Out of the blue, a piece of advice I had once given a young artist at a crucial time in her career came back to haunt me: "It's a tough road for those who dream and are prepared to go beyond dreaming. But to look back and know that one never tried to realize one's fondest dreams must be indescribably worse."

The old type A Cynthia had made a sudden appearance: I realized my fondest dream right at this moment was to break out of my straitjacket of fear.

"I won't tell them," I replied to my Very Sane Voice. "What I'll do is to prepare well. Have my points written down. Rest well in advance. Stay far away from the kind of thoughts that will trigger The Thing. I won't talk about the accident itself or the days immediately after. I know that's a Danger Zone."

~

Soon after arriving at the Oakville Conference Centre, I met Anne in person for the first time. We hugged. She took my bag then walked me to my table – her table. The other women there were welcoming, friendly. And very well dressed.

Part trade show, part motivational conference, part how-to workshop, this conference attracts business-women to learn and share with one another. Powerful, impressive women, aiming and reaching higher.

In their company, I thought, a person could feel brave without even trying. Which was good, since the theme of my panel was about finding the courage to get oneself through tough times. Or, in my case, one big event (a car accident) followed by a lengthy series of challenges.

Truth is, I had been so scared of talking about my journey of the last several years that I had even sidestepped radio and TV opportunities to promote my book.

As if my dirty little secret, PTSD, weren't bad enough, there was chronic pain – which is truly as awful as it sounds – and a head injury, which I didn't completely understand.

In my younger days, those last nine words would have made me laugh at the unintended irony.

The PTSD lurked inside my mind along with the thing that plagued my body: severe pain in my left shoulder and neck and all the way from my back right down to my right foot. Together, they changed my whole life.

I still wasn't sleeping well. I still wasn't conversing well. And I didn't willingly put myself in situations where the PTSD or the combined impact of the head injury and chronic pain could flatten me in front of others.

~

This panel, though, was meant to help and strengthen other women. That's ultimately why I had said yes. That's why I showed up to keep my promise.

You can do this, I told myself. It used to be second nature. And you are very well prepared.

I was determined to be courageous. After all, if you can't take a risk of front of women who take big risks every day ...

But I didn't want to embarrass myself, and I didn't want to embarrass these women. Above all, I didn't want to cause a panic. I wanted to make sure the worst symptoms of PTSD didn't emerge.

～

It happened every time I slept long enough to dream: my mind and body relived the accident – night terrors that woke me up, heart pounding.

Accidents in which my loved ones were killed. Sometimes I died, too.

In nine years, I had only five dreams that weren't nightmares. Five. I knew because I noted every good dream in my journals, describing them with pleasure immediately after I awoke.

My waking hours were somewhat better than the nights I slept, but only because I tried desperately to control my thoughts. As I told Sarah, my therapist, I carefully monitored what I was thinking almost all the time, like someone walking a tightrope who cannot afford to look away for even a second.

Still, the anxiety attacks hit without warning. An ordinary conversation could swiftly become a descent into hell. It didn't matter how many times it happened – while it was going on, I was sure I wouldn't escape. When it was over, both my body and mind felt beaten up, wrung out, useless.

The key was to avoid conversations, thoughts, or experiences that could lead to a subconscious flashback to the accident. And so I was always on guard, always carrying a little bag of invisible tools, in case of trouble.

One new tool was to acknowledge the problem to someone else. I had done this exactly twice: both times with a small group of people who had read my book and loved it. I wasn't embarrassed because they already knew I had PTSD and memory problems. Both were mentioned in A Good Home.

~

"A ship in harbour is safe," John A. Shedd noted, "but that is not what ships are built for."

I had left the harbour and was way out in the ocean. It was too late to turn back.

The moderator asked the first question and called my name. "What is the biggest challenge you have had to face?"

I gulped.

I told the audience I lived with chronic pain and "a nasty little thing called post-traumatic stress disorder."

They stared at me.

I told them I had learned some tools, one of them knowing when to "suddenly take a sharp left turn away from what I was saying" by completely changing the subject for a while.

"It's my way of managing," I said. "Of putting myself on firm ground when I'm feeling wobbly. No need to worry."

You could have heard a pin drop.

I wasn't sure what my revelation did for them, but it calmed my mind. I relaxed a little.

I was doing well, perhaps even very well. I was following my notes. I knew I had to mention the accident, but I also knew I couldn't afford to think back to it for long. So I said it all started with a car accident ... and I prepared to move on to the next point.

I was still feeling fine.

And ...

And then, out of the blue, I felt the strange-familiar sensation. Whatever was coming at me hadn't clobbered me yet, but I could almost glimpse it ... like a truck carrying a ticking bomb.

My stomach clenched, my heart sped up, and suddenly I was fighting back with everything I had. I desperately held myself in, afraid that, if I didn't, I would leak toxins into everybody in the room.

I could almost see them retreating in shock.

And then I remembered my invisible bag of tools. And my therapist's instructions: Keep your eyes wide open. Do NOT close your eyes. Look someone else in the eye. Breathe. Just breathe.

In the front row, the face of a woman with short blonde hair came into focus. She beamed encouragement at me. I looked her right in the eyes.

At that moment, I remembered what I told the audience but had forgotten: At some point, I might have to take a sharp left turn, talk about nothing in particular.

That moment was here now.

~

I think I talked about the weather.

I think I talked about the fact that I went into the men's washroom, not the ladies', which had a long lineup, but that I called out first, to make sure no men were inside. (It was a women's conference, after all.)

I think the audience laughed.

But I'm not sure.

~

Luckily, the moderator asked the next speaker, Charmaine, to answer the same question. And I continued the breathing exercises Sarah taught me.

Breathe in deeply, breathe out slowly. Repeat. Keep doing it. Now, focus on a happy image. Stay there. Eyes open. Remember to breathe …

The two women to my right were telling powerful, inspiring stories. I heard them, from a distance. Sometimes, I even understood. When I did, I nodded at their remarks, recognizing the truth, the power, in their words.

But I didn't always hear them. I was trying hard to use my tools and to control my trembling.

I briefly considered excusing myself and leaving. Or just running – okay, limping – out of the room. But I didn't. I felt glued to the chair.

When my turn came again, I talked about the fact that courage – like success – shouldn't be measured just in huge achievements but also in the small steps that make up the journey.

At least, this was what my notes said. This is what I'd planned to say. But I'm not sure if I said it.

The session ended. A stream of women headed toward me. The blonde woman with the reassuring face approached me. "Thank you for sharing your story," I think she said.

She was a pastor, she told me, and I found myself not at all surprised. She said more, and I heard it, and was glad she continued speaking to me.

I gave her my card. I wanted this exchange to matter, but I knew I wouldn't remember it; I was still only half there. I was working too hard to protect myself, to hold myself in, to allow anything else to have an impact.

Several other women came to talk to me.

Two women, Keisha and Nancy, came to my side. One or both gathered my belongings. Took me to say goodbye to Anne. Asked me to leave some books for sale. I stayed long enough to sign them.

As if feeling my extreme vulnerability, Nancy stayed close. Still holding my belongings, she walked with me to the waiting car. I thanked her.

My long-time friend Pamela – I hadn't realized she was there – approached and said something comforting. I tried to answer.

Still holding my belongings, Nancy walked me to my car. I thanked her.

I got inside, trembling, and let the tears flow for a good long while.

Chapter Thirty-three

Courage in Its Different Forms

Back at home, I changed into my pyjamas and headed straight to bed.

My mind and body felt as if they had been through a war. Which, in a way, they had.

Time had no meaning on such days. It must have been hours later when I finally forced myself to get up, determined to do something useful. To be normal.

I cooked dinner for Hamlin and Lauren, who came to visit. I said little. When I talked, the words came out in stutters, and at any rate, I really had to focus on what I was doing, so I wouldn't cut or burn myself.

I looked down at my body and realized I had forgotten to change out of my pyjamas.

But you cooked dinner, I thought. That's a small triumph.

Neither Hamlin nor Lauren tried to get me to talk during dinner. Then we watched TV. Or rather, I watched them watch TV.

And my heart filled with gratitude for these two people who loved me. And who understood.

～

I wasn't sure if Anne knew that accepting her invitation was a small act of courage on my part. And that walking on to that stage would be yet another.

I doubt if she knew that getting through the session would require courage bigger than those two acts combined. A desperate kind of courage, strengthened by careful planning.

When the scary moment came, I used almost every tool my therapist taught me:

When you get that strange feeling, don't tell yourself it's not happening. Trust yourself.
Keep your eyes open.
Breathe deeply. Breathe out slowly.
Try to switch your thoughts to something cheerful.
Keep your eyes open. Focus on one person's face if you can.
Breathe deeply. Breathe out slowly.

It sounds like a lot of little things, one after the other, for a period that likely lasted only seconds. But sometimes, as I think I told the women that day, courage is measured in the small steps we take.

~

I doubled the usual dose of painkillers and went to bed. My whole body was sore, my mind and emotions drained. The medication, combined with my exhaustion, helped. I sank gratefully into sleep.

Asleep and unable to defend myself, the nightmare came back with a vengeance. As if to say: "You escaped earlier, but now I'm in charge, and you have no tools to fight me."

~

The setting changes, but the narrative is essentially the same.

This time, I'm driving a large car and my whole family is inside it. We're talking and laughing, when – before I know it – the gentle slope becomes a steep cliff.

I'm unable to stop the car. I'm driving right over the cliff, plunging the car and my loved ones into a dark, bottomless space. The horror inside the car is real, intense, overwhelming.

～

The nightmare woke me up. My sheets were wet. Not with sweat, not with my tears. I had wet the bed.

My humiliation, thank God, was private this time. I had suspected it would be a rough night so had decided to sleep in the small bedroom next door.

I got up like a robot. Stripped the sheets and protective covering from the mattress. Walked unsteadily to the bathroom, placed them in the bath, and turned on the tap. I started washing the sheets and mattress cover.

Damn. Damn, damn, damn.

～

The older I got, and the more worries I had to deal with, the more I realized: everyone is struggling with something.

To be alive is to be exposed, someone once said. No one is immune.

A woman who approached me after the panel session was deeply worried about loved ones. Her close friend's husband was in bad shape after a car accident. It had been a long recovery period, and it wasn't over yet. The wife didn't know what to do.

"What would you advise?" she asked. "I mean, for the wife to do."

"She needs counselling," I replied. "And if possible, a support group. Her family doctor should find her one, or refer her to a social worker who will find the right one. Caregivers must take care of themselves, too."

I told her how relieved I was when my husband finally returned to cycling, cross-country skiing, and a more balanced diet. That I'd been worried about what would become of him. Caregivers often get ill but are so focused on the patient, they don't realize until it's too late.

"She must get help for herself," I said. Or, rather, that's what I would have said. But, as the woman spoke, tears came to her eyes then to mine. We were both choked up, and I knew I was hanging on by a thread.

"Please call me," I said, handing her my card. "Not sure I'm making sense now, so please call me."

~

Later, I thought about the courage of that man, working hard to recover but feeling trapped and wondering if he would ever get better.

About the courage of his wife, who was giving so much but was herself drowning.

And the courage of their close friend, who approached a stranger at a conference to seek advice.

~

At home the next morning, Lauren made me a cup of coffee. I gratefully accepted it.

She and her father were still not asking me any questions. But they were sticking close to home, caring without hovering. I walked down to the garden then noticed Hamlin seated on the verandah sipping his own coffee.

"Walk with me," I said.

He still didn't ask me the questions undoubtedly on his mind, and I still didn't offer any answers. The garden was peaceful and the air fresh and clean after the rain last evening. Neither of us wanted to interrupt this lovely moment.

He showed me the garden beds he had been working on, places where the huge old evergreen shrubs that surrounded our farmhouse had died over the winter. He had removed the branches in recent days and now had almost finished digging out the stumps from the earth. Next, he would bring in soil and compost and start planting.

"I'm going to move those two burning bush shrubs from the side garden," he said. "Put one in each bed here."

I nodded approval, knowing he would have to do it by himself, and feeling regretful about it. In the past, we would have done these tasks together.

"Let's go over to the arbour," I said.

Every spring, around this time, the arbour's trellised sides and roof were usually covered with clematis vines about to bloom.

We looked down at the spots where two vigorously healthy clematis vines once grew. It had been a harsh winter – thick snow covered the ground for four months – and the area's wild rabbits were denied access to their normal sources of winter food. So they ate our clematis vines down to the ground, and even in mid-spring there wasn't even a bit of green to be seen in the spots where these flowering vines once grew.

But now we spied green stems shooting up from the ground in two spots. The young vines looked remarkably strong.

Hamlin and I gasped with surprise and delight.

"Unbelievable that neither the hungry rabbits nor the harsh winter killed them," I said. "And now they're making a brand-new start! Wow!"

Wonder lit his face. "Yes. Everything died. But underground, the roots stayed alive."

We smiled at the plants and each other and slowly headed back to the house.

~

Courage comes in all forms.

On my most recent visit to the hospital, just weeks before the conference in June, my specialist, Dr. Helen, had said she was concerned about my immune system. She instructed me to stay away from crowds, do my therapeutic exercises at home, and start seeing a counsellor again regularly.

It was her second warning in six months. Back in November, she had determined that my recovery had relapsed. She had put me under a kind of house arrest back then, too.

I had felt my decline happening, saw it happening, and felt helpless to fight it. The few times I ventured outside the house during that brutal winter, I came back in with a virus of one kind or another. By the end of March, I could feel myself drifting away, my body becoming weary, my spirit becoming lethargic.

By the time I showed up for my regular appointment at the hospital, I felt ashamed.

"I take full responsibility," I told Dr. Helen before she could respond. "I can put up a fight against the endless pain, the PTSD, and the lack of sleep. But add two other illnesses at the same time, and I keel over. Like a ... like a leaf in a breeze."

"Stop blaming yourself."

Her voice was stern, but I thought I caught a glint of warmth in her eyes. She knew my expectations of myself were sometimes way too high.

"All my patients who have complex injuries had a very rough winter. Now the good weather is here ..." She eyed me more seriously this time. "You have to be careful."

And then she had told me what I needed to do, and I had taken careful notes. And promised to do everything she said.

~

Lauren took time away from work to help me through the following weeks.

We exercised together each morning. Then I had a hot bath and rest. I was not allowed to visit my computer.

People like me take forever to establish a new habit. Sarah had told me it goes with the PTSD territory.

But Lauren was determined to break my habit of going to the computer whenever I got worried. She knew sitting at the computer for more than half an hour at a time would only increase my pain, and then I'd be so worn out I wouldn't have the energy to exercise.

She knew I had to break that pattern. Every night and early morning, she hid the computer mouse.

~

"Did you think I was wrong to take part in the conference yesterday?" I asked Lauren when I finished my exercises the first day.

"No! I know it was painful, but I think you had to do it."

"Sometimes, I don't know my limits unless I come right up against them. What happened taught me that I still have a lot of work to do."

"True."

"But ... I took that sharp left turn! I sensed something was wrong, and I took that left turn before everything went crazy. It could have been a lot worse, but I took the left turn."

"I'm so proud of you, Mom."

"Thank you for encouraging me ... with these exercises and everything."

"You're welcome."

I could hear the smile in her voice.

A companionable silence followed.

"Is it getting more bearable now?" she asked.

"Yes," I said, without asking whether she meant the exercises or my recovery from the previous day's events.

~

A couple hours later, Hamlin said, "I'm going to the store to pick up some herbs. Wanna come with me?"

It was a rare request. I still took a long time to get dressed, and with time at a premium, he usually headed out on short errands by himself.

Surprised, I said yes.

We were driving to the store when he asked, "How did it go?"

"I honestly don't know. I had good notes. I know there were some good points in those notes. But did I say them? I don't know."

"I'm sure you did."

"I particularly wanted to talk about the fact that, sometimes, one has to see courage and success in a new way – not just by the big, glorious victories, but by the small steps that we take, the small achievements."

"I'm sure you made an impact. Your story makes an impact."

"Hmm ..." I answered quietly. Reassured, but not entirely.

~

I realized that, in the last few weeks, I had seen courage take different forms.

Anne putting me on stage at her conference, although she had read my book and knew that I had a few problems.

A woman approaching me on behalf of her friends who were in an awful state.

My daughter deciding to take time away from work to help me through this time.

And my husband waiting until the right moment to ask me the question he must have been dying to ask.

~

The mouse was back in its place. I saw a message in my email Inbox.

I was so inspired by your message and courage yesterday.

Thank you for your transparency and bravery speaking with us and helping me to look at the definition of success differently.

Best wishes as you continue on your journey to wellness and I am looking forward to reading your book!

Kindest regards,
Tracy

~

Courage comes in different forms and affects each of us differently.

This is what I thought after I read that note from Tracy. Sometimes, you have to push yourself to do a thing, no matter how frightened you feel. You know it may help only one person. That what you do or say may matter to only one person. But you do it anyway.

Sometimes, the person you reach is a total stranger.

And sometimes that person is yourself.

Chapter Thirty-four

Running Away to Home

I had been tempting the fates, and I knew it. Pushing the limits in several different ways. But after a fall and winter spent mostly in bed, I was tired of writing in my journals, tired of my blog, tired of my cloistered life.

I wanted to run away but wanted the shelter of my home at the same time.

It was like that time in my adolescence when I ran away – all the way to my grandmother's house nearby. My friends all thought that was ridiculous.

"If you really want to run away, you don't go to Granny's house!" they said.

My version of running away this time was to set up residence on our verandah. Strange that I had lived here in this home for nearly nine years but hadn't truly enjoyed the verandah. Now, it became my headquarters.

Being there meant I could be in the garden, enjoy the warm weather, but not feel tempted to help Hamlin. Most of his gardening work was in the back or front yard, and this verandah faced the side yard, where perennials jostled for space with each other but required little care.

So, out came the brightly coloured cushions in different shades of blue and a soft red. They brightened up the white-stained wooden Muskoka chairs, built for comfort.

Out came the old wicker chairs, bought decades before and in need of freshening up. I dusted them off, told myself they looked perfect, and added a cushion to each one.

Out came the old, partially threadbare Persian rug in tones of deep reds and blues. Hamlin placed it in the centre, between the chairs. Then he spread small wicker tables that looked like boxes amidst the furniture.

The outdoor table had been left on the verandah over the winter. It was plastic and showed its old age.

I slowly washed it then searched inside for a rugged white tablecloth that would fit its large rectangular size. My eye caught the old white chenille spread that should have been thrown out when we moved but had been forgotten. It had two fair-sized holes at one end.

Aha! It would make the perfect tablecloth.

And it did.

With our long white wooden bench and wicker chairs and love seat around the covered table, the verandah suddenly became an outdoor room in which I could sit when I needed, lie down when I got tired, or do nothing at all.

It took me several days to do all this, but I did it. And it had cost me nothing but a bit of effort.

～

Il dolce far niente, the Italians call it: the sweetness of doing nothing.

I never knew what it was like to sit and do nothing but enjoy the act of sitting – or lying still. PTSD had made me perennially anxious; I always found something to do when I had nothing to do. Read. Write. Dust the furniture. Anything to avoid flashbacks and worries.

Yes, I loved walking in the garden and discovering new developments. The flowers in bud. The ones that had just bloomed. The ones I had completely forgotten.

But I had never known what it was like to enjoy the garden without worrying about it. Indeed, after Hamlin caught me in the act that day, I still found it difficult to walk through the garden without succumbing to guilt over all the work he had to do without my help.

~

Dr. Helen had firmly ruled out a return to the therapy pool at Toronto Rehab.

"The hot water pool? No! Your immune system is weak, and pools and changing-room areas are a prime place to pick up germs."

So we had settled instead on daily exercises, which included physiotherapy and walking around the garden up to five times each day.

Hamlin noticed my distress one day as I stopped my walk and surveyed the garden.

"Don't even think about it," he said. "Keep walking."

But one day he said, "Come and show me a few things you want done in the garden."

I was relieved, even thrilled. I meekly followed him. "I'll show you the easiest things."

"No. Show me the things that need the most attention."

"Okay, then!" I said, looking around.

My spirits sank. There was so much to do, so much I would have done by myself, that I didn't know where to start.

"Ummm ..."

Hamlin waited.

We finally decided on a few things, starting with a few perennials that had outgrown their spot and needed moving to somewhere else.

"Where do you want them?" he asked, businesslike.

"Over there," I said, pointing to a bed on our left. "I can help you. I can water them, or ..."

"No! Just point and walk away."

I pointed, hovered, and, after being reminded yet again, walked away.

Hamlin would have to repeat that order several times through the spring.

It got to the stage where he would open his mouth and I would say, "I know. Just point and walk away." But by then, instead of feeling frustrated, I would smile.

He never showed it, but I suspected that, inwardly, Hamlin was smiling, too. I had finally learned my lesson.

~

I returned to the verandah each time to rest until the next garden walk.

There were things to do inside the house, and I gladly did them. The dishes. The laundry. The dusting. Offering Hamlin a cold drink or a snack. Making lunch or dinner, or both.

The more of my duties that Hamlin took over in the garden, the more I showed my appreciation by keeping him fed. Some meals still turned out badly, but most were at least edible, and a few were even tasty. Hamlin loved to grill chicken, fish, and vegetables on the barbecue, so when he got tired of my paltry efforts, he would fire it up.

I realized one day I hadn't been writing in my journals, and that meant I hadn't been making optimal use of the verandah. Nor had we been taking advantage of the table and chairs we had placed in one corner.

"I'd like us to have some meals out there," I told Hamlin one Saturday. "Have lunch with me after your bike ride today."

There we were, with a wonderful verandah that

wrapped around most of the house, yet we had rarely enjoyed it.

~

"I've taken to the verandah," I said to anyone who phoned me.

The words had a magical effect.

Relatives and friends whom I hadn't seen in many months were suddenly inviting themselves to visit. It was as if they had been waiting for me to utter the words that would indicate I was ready for visitors, after the long hard winter I'd been through.

And, at any rate, doesn't everyone love a verandah?

It was the summer of visits.

Some came for tea or lunch then left reluctantly.

Some came for lunch and lingered until supper.

And some came for supper and visited until late in the evening.

~

My friend Tim was returning home to South Africa after nearly forty years in Canada. Most of his last week before travelling was spent at the farmhouse with our family.

He held court on the verandah like an éminence grise, saying wise, cryptic, and funny things to everyone who dropped in.

Some of our visitors wondered how he would handle returning to a country he had left decades earlier.

Tim's enigmatic reply: "Did I mention I'll have the use of a heated swimming pool?"

"Long way to go for a heated swimming pool," one of us said.

Tim and I had agreed on a fair exchange of value: he could stay in my home if he promised to praise my cooking at every opportunity.

The weather was perfect, and we had breakfast, lunch, and supper on the verandah that week. On the very first night of Tim's visit, I made a cauliflower and cheese dish. The dish called for only two ingredients, but I somehow forgot to add one of them, the cheese. It tasted horrible.

"You are the best cook I've ever met," Tim declared, straight-faced, to loud laughter from everyone at the table.

I swatted him with my dinner napkin. In return, he complained theatrically of "the abuses" he suffered in my home.

This was how we dealt with what would be a wrenching farewell.

It was Tim who had recruited me from journalism school then helped guide my television career at the Canadian Broadcasting Corporation. Over the years, he had gone from mentor to dear friend. In the post-accident periods when I stuttered then cried at least once during every conversation, he had shown a patience I never knew he possessed.

It was Tim who did the first edit of the manuscript that would become *A Good Home*. He had stuck with me throughout the long process – even on days when I was incoherent.

South Africa was so far away, I feared I would never see him again. But I was determined to not show my sadness. Tim had given me so much over the years; the one thing I knew I could give him was a pleasant and comfortable last week in Canada.

Every so often, Tim and I would stop to marvel at our good fortune: to relax on a verandah, with trees and flowers, birds and butterflies nearby, and in the precious company of an old friend.

~

How can a person have lived in a house with such a splendid verandah and not enjoyed it before? I often wondered during that spring and summer.

I knew the answers: I'd been in too much pain. I'd been too tense, always walking the tightrope that helped keep the anxiety attacks at bay. I'd been too furious at it all. But I'd also been too afraid to find joy: afraid of the future, afraid of the present, afraid of the past.

Taking to the verandah was an act of faith, an act of trust. A covenant not only with God and nature but also with myself.

It became part of my daily schedule of exercise, housework, and rest. And it taught me to sit still and enjoy my house in a way that did not involve work.

I was finally learning what the therapists at Toronto Rehab had tried to teach me.

~

I had told the therapists there that I was failing meditation 101.

"Meditation isn't something you can fail," they replied.

But you should at least get something out of it, I thought.

I desperately wanted to rid myself of the natter in my mind that everything that had happened was my fault.

You wouldn't know that I wasn't the one driving the car that crashed into mine.

It was my fault that the nightmares plagued me. It had to be because my personality had been so driven, so totally type A. That's also why I hadn't surrendered to the injuries soon enough, had fought too hard against them for too long, had refused to believe I had PTSD.

It was my fault that the pain was so intense. After all, a recent study said redheads feel pain more acutely, and while my hair had turned brown decades ago, I had been a redhead for most of my childhood.

Vanity, thy name is Cynthia. Vanity had led me to the false assumption that, if I tried hard enough, I would not fail. And it was vanity that made me cringe whenever I saw my future self in a wheelchair, or even using a walker.

Meanwhile, other people in the darkened room at Toronto Rehab responded to the guided meditation with what seemed like absolute peace. Some even snored softly, while I lay awake, listening to my quarrelsome thoughts.

~

"Everybody needs beauty as well as bread," John Muir proclaimed. "Places to play in and pray in where nature may heal and give strength to body and soul."

In earlier years, almost all of my time in the garden had been spent working. After the accident, most of my time there was spent regretting the chores I could no longer do.

Playing? No.

Now, as I sat on the verandah, I realized that it's hard to enjoy a garden when you're running around trying to fix or perfect it. By its very nature, a garden defies such efforts, by changing and growing in its own perfectly imperfect way. All the armies of gardeners and their tools and nutrients cannot guarantee a perfect garden.

To truly enjoy it, to soak in its beauty, to learn its greatest lessons, you have to learn the art of stillness. Not just the outward appearance of stillness, where your body is unmoving but your mind races a mile a minute, worrying about this and that and whatnot.

Between the flow of visitors that late spring and summer, in that space between the exercises and the housework, between answering the phone and worrying about the bills, a funny thing happened: I learned to sit still.

So still that each cricket chirp stood out from the symphony around it.

So still that a bird sat quietly on the Muskoka chair opposite me, waiting its turn at the feeder nearby.

So still that, when it rained, I felt sure I could have counted the raindrops … if I wanted.

One day, a butterfly floated near my face. I slowly turned my head to follow its movement, and when it disappeared, I patiently waited for its return.

Another time, a rabbit took a diagonal shortcut across the lawn by running right past my feet.

An ant once carried a large feather across the verandah floor; I watched it for several long minutes, wondering how an insect that small could carry something so big.

In the garden, every flower became its own gorgeous portrait.

Sitting or lying still on that verandah, taking in the smells, the sights, the movements of small creatures – these were moments of exquisite, perhaps even sacred, beauty.

I would sometimes reach a state where my body and mind seemed to float above the pain for whole chunks of time. This was what the therapists at Toronto Rehab had meant when they taught us the pain-relieving effects of mindfulness and meditation. I was finally learning it, not in a hospital room, but on the verandah of our home.

Chapter Thirty-five

The Return to Dr. Helen

I t wasn't a long wait this time.

I flipped through the magazine I'd brought for this purpose: a way of passing the usual thirty minutes or so before the doctor called me into her examining room at the hospital.

I dutifully padded behind her down the long white corridor, my shoes and rubber-tipped cane barely audible against the shiny hard hospital floor. Into the room I followed her.

"I like that haircut," I said, once we were seated across from each other. "It suits you."

"Oh, I just had it done yesterday."

It was the first time we were relating as women, as equals of a sort. For years, she had been the expert doctor, and I had been the blubbering, stuttering, bleary-eyed patient – a human bundle of pain and confusion.

～

At home that morning, I had picked up a copy of the newest issue of *Arabella* magazine and written "To Dr. Helen" at the top of my newest feature story.

Now, I handed the magazine to her. "This is for you. This is the magazine that published the first stories my husband found. Those stories led to the book."

"I know. I have your book."

I remembered giving her a copy. I also remembered how I felt at that moment: desperate to say thanks, desperate to show her I was strong enough to complete a book. Desperate for a bit of respect.

She was the older woman I had thought I would become. Confident, knowledgeable, respected. Attractive, stylish, comfortable in her own skin.

Instead, my fifties had been a disaster and the Cynthia Reyes I had known had disappeared, along with dreams of the Cynthia Reyes I had planned to become.

"Beautiful!" she said, eyes wide. "I've never seen this magazine before."

"It's published four times a year."

She continued riffling through the pages. She found my story. "This is great! Did you take the photos, too?"

I laughed. "No way! But the editors did a great job with them, didn't they?"

~

For a moment I wondered what it must have been like for her to be my rehabilitation specialist: she had met me at my worst; my recovery had been agonizingly slow.

"Writing has been good for you," she said, raising her head from the magazine and holding my gaze.

"Yes."

"When did you start writing for the magazine?"

"A few years ago. Though most of the stories they published were written long ago. They were the first stories Hamlin found in old computers and bags and boxes."

"Yes," she said, remembering.

In the pause, I recalled an image of myself, the high achiever, leading a meeting of television professionals in Europe.

"I used to be a star, you know," I said softly. "Before."

I stared at my cane for a while as if it belonged to someone else.

"I travelled the world, making keynote presentations, training others, sharing ground-breaking ideas. When I talked, people listened. Then I ... I ... lost it all ... and ... people treated me very differently."

She nodded.

"I think that's why I kept trying so desperately to do everything the doctors requested – I didn't want to fail in front of them. But I felt dismissed by some doctors. And that just made everything worse. I could see that look in their eyes."

Dr. Helen didn't state the obvious: "But how would you know? You were in such a bad state."

"This will sound sexist," I continued. "But now I look back and realize ... it wasn't till I got an all-female team around me that I felt understood for the first time. You, my family doctor, my therapists ... you looked beyond the tears, the stuttering, the mishmash of words."

"It could also have been that some doctors don't know what to do in such an emotional situation," Dr. Helen said. "They just don't know what to say."

"I'm sure. But having grown up in an era where women had to prove themselves equal to men, it hurt me to find myself in situations where I was so clearly subordinate to them ... unequal."

I wasn't asking her to criticize her medical colleagues. I wasn't asking her to empathize with me. But there I was, in a small hospital room with a female doctor who seemed only a few years older than I, a woman I felt comfortable having such a discussion with.

In fact, it was the most lucid progression of thoughts I had ever shared with her.

In my pre-accident world, doctors had never been gods. To me, they were just another set of professionals who might be good at their work or not, and my interactions with them had been as their equal. I questioned their assessments, wanting to know how they arrived at them; questioned their prescriptions. In a few cases, I had even questioned their qualifications then made a teasing remark to remove the sting.

It was the journalist in me, the person who always brought a healthy dose of skepticism to interactions with those who occupied positions of authority.

It takes confidence – even power – to behave like that. But I was no longer a confident, powerful woman. I probably would never return to a state where I would feel truly equal to Dr. Helen or any other powerful professional. Still, we had just shared a lucid conversation in which I had done most of the talking.

I could feel myself getting choked up again. We needed to change the subject.

At that moment, Dr. Helen began her examination. "Push your foot against my hand, like this," she said, showing me what she meant.

Her demonstration was necessary, and I still had to think about what she was asking. Even on a good day, it was difficult for me to follow a simple set of instructions.

She detected a bit more strength in my right foot. I was thrilled.

"Now lift your right leg from the floor."

My foot and leg did not move.

"I ... I need to try that again."

Nothing.

"I need to try that again," I said, giving it all my might this time.

Still nothing. I was furious. "I've been exercising. I've been walking ... How can I walk if I can't raise my foot? I need to understand this! I need to understand these things."

I knew, of course, that walking is an entirely different task from raising one's leg while seated. I had struggled with this problem since the accident. I thought I had grown to accept that particular limitation. Apparently not.

I had to catch my breath and stop at several moments to keep from crying. But I held myself together. I had some bigger questions, and I needed answers.

Why my head sometimes hurt so badly when more than one person was talking.

Why I missed so much of what was said to me at times but could recall whole chunks of simple conversation at others.

How I could write a whole short story but not follow simple instructions or fill in a simple questionnaire without becoming frustrated.

I furiously jotted her replies in my notebook, often asking her to repeat what she had said.

Meanwhile, my right shoulder was inflamed. That I knew very well. It was my cane arm, because my left arm was unreliable. I leaned heavily on the cane to help myself up and down stairs, and sometimes just to move a few steps. My whole right side was very weak and needed the help, but I had not realized I was hurting my right shoulder until it was too late.

"I know you won't want to hear this," Dr. Helen said. She paused ever so slightly and looked me right in the eye.

No, I won't, I thought.

"A walker would take the pressure off your right shoulder ..."

I stared at her. I had not thought about a walker recently and did not want to think about it now.

"It would distribute the pressure between both shoulders."

Oh, God, I thought. A walker. My throat tightened. My eyes were getting teary. I swallowed hard. No bloody crying, I told myself. Get a grip.

I could see the sense in everything she said. But I could also visualize myself tottering around behind a walker, and the image was awful. It was not me, that image. It was a white-haired woman wearing an old cotton housedress, pushing a metal walker, slowly. Very slowly. She looked about to expire.

Oh, God.

~

My mother's words came to mind again: sometimes you just have to take the bad with the good and carry on.

Life was like that. Never a straight road, never entirely good or bad, but a mishmash of both. Medical appointments had been like this one ... except with more bad news than good. But I was spiritually stronger now. And I had the use of my words.

Out of my mouth came these words: "Last May, you told me to stay home because my immune system was so weak. But you also told me to walk around the grounds of my home as much as I could. So I walked at least five times a day, leaning on the cane. That's when my right shoulder started to hurt. So this is all your fault!"

"It's all my fault," Dr. Helen agreed, unruffled.

"I'm so glad to be finally able to blame you for something," I laughed. "But those walks were very good for me. To breathe fresh air, to walk frequently through the garden ... that was great, so I guess I have to blame you for that, too."

We smiled at each other.

"Are some walkers light?" I asked after a pause. "The ones I tried out some years ago were heavy."

"Yes, some are very light."

"Then I'll get one and use it whenever I walk … on our grounds. But I'm sorry: I still can't bring myself to use one in public. Not just yet."

I had told Dr. Helen I felt spiritually stronger. But that didn't mean I had lost all my vanity.

～

Dr. Helen had told me to read about a condition that impedes the body's ability to carry out the brain's orders. She sounded as if she had told me this before.

Had other doctors told me? Had Dr. Helen? I could not recall. I also suspected that my health-care professionals had given me only the information they thought I could handle at whatever stage I had reached. I dimly understood that and even appreciated it. A person has to be able to understand.

But you also have to want to understand, I thought.

I did not want to understand this.

～

Dr. Helen was talking to me about the movie *Still Alice*. About some lines by the lead character, played by actress Julianne Moore, who has developed Alzheimer's while in her early fifties: "Please do not think I am suffering. I am not suffering. I am struggling. Struggling to be a part of things – to stay connected to what I once was."

Still Alice was one of the first books I had listened to when reading print became difficult. I had had to hit "rewind" over and over, to concentrate on what I was hearing, to remember it before moving on, but still it was easier than reading.

At the time, I had marvelled at how closely Alice's symptoms resembled mine. Listening to the book scared me, yet I could not stop listening.

"You must keep writing," Dr. Helen was saying, and I realized I had missed some of what she had just said. "Writing is good for you. And keep reading your book to small groups, where you feel protected. It's good for you, too."

We had already gone beyond the time allotted for this visit. But a question was gnawing at my mind. I looked her straight in the eye.

"Will it come back? The bad times … of not being able to think or speak? Will they come back?"

Dr. Helen returned my look. "You are strong and you are brave. I want you to look at the possibility that, whatever comes, you'll handle it."

Part Three

A Stream Runs Through It

Chapter Thirty-six

A Tough Act to Follow

A reader telephoned one day that summer. "I just finished reading your book," he said. "I love it. It's like a movie. I hope someone turns it into a movie."

I'd heard this a dozen times or more, but this time it was just about the biggest compliment I could get. My caller worked in the media and was an expert on storytelling.

"My wife's been watching me read it. I've been totally absorbed in it, and now that I've finished, she wants to read it, too. But I don't think I'll let her."

"Why not?" I was puzzled and a bit crestfallen.

"That husband of yours makes it tough for other guys," he said with a laugh. "Next thing you know, she'll be expecting the same from me! I don't think I could live up to his example."

He was referring to my worst years after the accident, when each month seemed to bring only worse news about my injuries. Hamlin found himself doing his own work plus mine at both the office and home. Even in my bleary state, I could tell he was sometimes frightened. Never before in our marriage had we been faced with such a mighty, lengthy test.

Somehow, Hamlin managed. Somehow, he found strength, faith, and patience.

Now, it bothered me to think that someone who had read my book believed he wouldn't be able to overcome a similar challenge.

"How do you know that? You might surprise yourself."

In an email I sent him later that day, I told him, "Be assured that you, too, would rise to the big tests that life throws in your path. I think if you asked my husband, he might say he surprised himself with the courage and tenacity he's shown in these tough times."

Then I realized that I had never asked Hamlin myself. Since the accident, we had talked often about how I was doing. Now I needed him to talk about himself. I suspected it wouldn't be easy.

~

As we sat at the kitchen table having supper, I told Hamlin about my exchange with the reader.

"Do you think you've had to grow because of all this?" I asked. "With everything you've had to handle?"

"I've never thought about it," he said. "I think I must have. But you know me. What do you think?"

"You're gentler, and much more patient. And stronger."

"Are you saying I wasn't always a gentle and patient kinda guy?"

"Not always."

A few minutes later, I asked, "Did you surprise yourself?"

He put down his knife and fork. "I just did what I had to do."

"Were you frightened at times?"

"Absolutely."

"Have you ever thought of escaping?"

"Escaping?"

"Just running away from it all."

"No. I never have. And where would I run to?"

"Any place where there isn't an injured, dependent wife."

He stared at me, shocked. "It never even occurred to me."

We sipped our wine and continued eating. I changed tack. "You stopped teasing me, you know. As if you thought I was too fragile to be teased. But you've started again. And you're laughing more. I really like that."

Every so often, while we ate, one of us looked at the other and smiled. The silence was like a warm blanket. Soft, yet sturdy and sure.

Chapter Thirty-seven

A Good Man

Fear should get more respect. Without it, who would need courage?

I wasn't joking when I asked Hamlin if he had ever thought of leaving me during our toughest times. I had learned from other people who had suffered long-term injuries, and I knew that, in some cases, marriages deteriorated into divorce.

Was it because the caregiving partner felt overwhelmed? Or was it also fear?

I had seen the fear in Hamlin's eyes. It had pierced my heart to see this brave man, this strong man, grappling with his fears on my behalf. Worse, those were the times when I lacked the words to comfort him.

Over and over, I counted my blessings that he had found the courage to stay. I had no doubt: a different man would have left me.

～

We had raised our two children together, bought and sold several homes together, taken part in a variety of charitable projects in our community.

We had built careers in the television industry, all

the while supporting each other. We had helped each other to grow in our work and as human beings. I knew it, he knew it, and we used our experience to advise our older daughter Nikisha before and after she and Tim got married.

"We end up helping to raise our husbands," I told Nikisha one day. "And they also help to raise us. It's a rare person who comes into a marriage fully formed."

Her father nodded. Like other couples, we had been through rough times. But our mutual love and encouragement had undoubtedly made us a stronger couple.

"You'll bring certain strengths and certain weaknesses to the marriage," Hamlin said. "Same for Tim."

"The key is to shore up your partner where he is weak," I added. "Without ever humiliating the other person. You may become frustrated at times, but never shame each other about weaknesses."

~

Marriage, I knew, is the closest of all adult relationships. What other relationship demands that two adults share the same bed, the same room, the same bank account, the same life?

And because of that closeness, that dependency on each other, the partners usually expect understanding. When it's absent, the bonds of the relationship can become painfully strained.

This, too, Hamlin and I had learned the hard way. We had seen how an impatient word, carelessly uttered, can devastate someone who loves you.

Our opinions of each other, our respect and patience with each other, mattered profoundly.

These things we shared with our daughter, hoping they would help, yet knowing that making mistakes is the way we humans learn while our brains and wisdom are taking time to develop. Nikisha and Tim would make their own mistakes and learn their own lessons.

~

Now, as I faced the losses of recent years, and the strain it had put on my husband, I wondered how much longer he could continue. Was there a limit to the patience one person could have for another's many weaknesses?

Was there a limit to love?

Every financial plan we had made was predicated on my being an equal income earner, and this decade had been identified as the period in which – having supported our parents, schooled our children, paid for one wedding, and donated to charities – we would make the money needed to finance our retirement years.

I had tried to work after the accident, and I did at times. But it was anyone's guess how I would manage from one day to the next. Would I be able to walk tomorrow, or sit, or stand? Would I be able to hold a single thought in my head? Would I be able to speak coherently?

Unfortunately, the kind of work I did required all of the above. Hamlin finally asked me to stop. It was causing everyone too much stress, he said. And worse, he couldn't stand to see my frustration at all the things I no longer could do.

"Just focus on getting better," he had said. "Leave everything else to me."

And so, for the last several years, he had been our only breadwinner.

The burden had taken its toll. I could see it in his hair, now gone completely grey. I could see it in the lines on his face. I could tell by the number of nights he left our bed, unable to sleep.

~

Without wanting to, without meaning to, I had caused my family such grief, and my husband most of all.

And now, the place where he felt most sheltered and comfortable – his home – had turned into a place of pain and uncertainty.

How much longer before he would have to sell the house? He wouldn't say, as if discussing it would sap his strength. But worry about the possibility often kept me awake.

I didn't know which was worse: to take the prescribed painkillers and be ravaged by PTSD-related nightmares or decline the pills and be ravaged by my fears for the future.

But deep down I always knew this much: I had been blessed with a good man, and he was not the kind to leave me behind.

Chapter Thirty-eight

It's Always Something

"Into every life a little rain must fall," my mother was fond of saying when I hit a speed bump and overreacted.

But I never expected it to fall inside my house.

One day, I turned on the kitchen faucet the way I always did. But this time it spewed water from all the wrong places. Water all over the countertop and onto my clothes.

"Help!" I yelled. "The kitchen tap's gone nuts!"

Husband came running down the stairs. Turned off the water supply, grabbed his toolbox, started dismantling things.

Half an hour later, I thought I heard a swear word from under the sink. Followed by another. Along with a series of gasps and grunts and other unhappy sounds.

Frustrated, he grabbed his car keys and headed to the hardware store. Came back clutching some small, unidentified chrome things in a clear plastic bag.

"The guy at the store gave these to me," he explained tersely. "But he wasn't sure they'd work."

The guy at the store was right.

Several days later, we were still washing bowls, pots,

strainers, and large cutlery in the laundry room tub, waiting for the faucet parts to arrive in the mail.

"This reminds me of my early childhood!" I said, trying to lighten the mood. "We had to pour water into a big tub on a table in an outside room and wash all the dishes in it."

Home, back then, meant a tiny pink four-room farmhouse. I remembered standing on a wooden stool and feeling like a big girl as I took my turn washing the dishes. Our family had none of the conveniences I now blithely took for granted – back then I didn't even know that such things as dishwashers existed.

But Hamlin thought I was romanticizing the hardships of my childhood. As far as he was concerned, there was nothing romantic in this day and age about being inconvenienced like this.

～

The parts finally arrived, and Hamlin set to fixing the faucet. This time, there were no swear words from under or above the sink. The grunts I heard were ones of satisfaction.

But before we could properly say a prayer of thanks, the clothes dryer went on the blink. Literally: blinking lights appeared on the panel. But no heat inside the machine.

The lady at the 1-800 customer service number said it would be nearly a week before they could get a repairman to our home.

"At least the washing machine still works," I said to Hamlin, trying to console him and myself.

So we washed our clothes and hung them to air dry on upright radiators in every room in the house.

"Aren't we glad we have radiators and not those air

registers in the floor?" I said, wringing a silver lining out of the situation.

My good man nodded in agreement, but didn't smile. To him, one gadget breaking down was bad enough. But two? Within just a few days?

When we ran out of room on the radiators, we hung the clothes over metal chairs on the verandah. We even spread some towels on the large juniper bushes that sprawled just outside the kitchen door.

But our bad luck hadn't run its course. Now the dishwasher stopped working. Oh, it ran the water through, all right. And made the usual noises. But after all the sound and fury, the dishes were dirty and filmy, cups still coffee-stained, forks and spoons gritty with specks of food still on them. Ugghhh!

I unpacked every dirty dish, cup, bowl, knife, fork, and spoon and washed them all by hand.

With three conveniences out of order in just over a week, we agreed a good strong coffee was in order.

Hamlin reached for the coffee machine and took the necessary steps. Filled the container with water. Made sure enough coffee beans were in place. Pressed the button over a cup.

Dark brown fluid spouted through the side and bottom of our once reliable coffee maker, flooding the counter space around the machine.

The darned thing was also on the fritz.

The faucet, the dryer, the dishwasher, the coffee maker. Our kitchen was old and looked it. There were no granite counters, no top-of-the-line Wolfe or Dacor stoves, no Sub Zero fridges to be found here.

Our newer appliances were bought only after repairmen had inspected their broken predecessors, shaken their heads grimly, and said words like, "Yes, this one has definitely given up the ghost!" Or: "I could take your money, but this thing is so outdated it would be a crime to try to fix it."

One by one, we bought replacements at a store that gave steep discounts on appliances that had been dented during shipping. Still, how could all four things have stopped working just days apart?

It was as if some angel, bored out of his skull from all that good-doing, decided to make some mischief. And chose our home.

Hamlin and I stared at each other in disbelief. He finally started to laugh. "It's always something," he said.

"And if it's not something, it's something else," I added.

Chapter Thirty-nine

Hamlin the Undercover Cop

It was mid-afternoon, and I was sitting in one of my favourite places: Vito and Loretta's kitchen, around the corner from my home.

I hadn't seen Vito and Loretta in several weeks.

Vito and I sipped our wine, because that's what he offered when you came to his house after midday. Not espresso, not cappuccino – just wine, made by his own hands.

The wine was so strong I was sure just a few large sips would scour out my insides. But these were two of my most favourite neighbours. And, when in an Italian home, I decided, I must do what the Italians do. So I always accepted the wine.

I took very small sips from the huge glass Vito handed me.

"How's Hamlin?" he asked. "And your daughters?"

"Everyone's fine, thanks, Vito."

"I still miss my friend Kinu."

"So do I. We all miss him. Sometimes, I turn a corner in the house and expect to see him there. He was such a sweet dog."

"You see ..." Vito often started like this when he was

about to make a wise observation. "You see … some people don't realize that a dog can be big and yet gentle. Kinu was a gentle dog. He was a gentleman!"

"That he was," I said, raising my glass to Vito's to toast the giant Akita who had died two years earlier. Our neighbours, taken aback by this huge, furry creature, had stood back at first, more appraising than approving. But Kinu had quickly made many friends in our neighbourhood, starting with Paddy and Vito and the neighbourhood children.

"And how's the book? People buying your book?" Vito asked.

"Yes, they are. Have you read it yet?"

Vito looked slightly embarrassed. "Well … I read the chapters about myself first …"

"But of course. I'd do the same. Did you still like what I wrote?"

"Of course I like it. You did a very good job. Now I have to go back and start the book and read it from the beginning."

"No pressure, Vito. But there will be a test on what you've read … Next week!"

This time, Loretta, who was doing something at the kitchen counter, joined in the laughter.

～

Vito hauled a thick book off the shelf. A long time ago, this shelf was meant to house plates or cups or glasses, but over the years, Vito's books had taken over more and more space.

Loretta told me she had gotten used to it but still threatened him with, "You bring one more book into this kitchen and I'll throw it out!"

I sneaked a look at Loretta, who was rolling her eyes affectionately at her husband.

While many of Vito's friends would discuss wine and gardening, few were given to reading thick books or talking about them. It was one of the reasons Loretta liked my visits: I genuinely liked to learn about the books Vito was reading.

The book had a full-page collage of black-and-white photos of people who came to Canada, or lived in Canada, around the time Vito moved here permanently from southern Italy. The faces were distinctive, each one inviting a second look.

"Did you notice this one, Vito?" I asked, angling the picture back toward him and pointing to the face of a middle-aged man. "Who does it remind you of?"

Vito peered at it, and, in his own Vito fashion, said nothing for a moment. Then he squinted and moved closer to the picture.

"A little bit like my father," he said at last.

"A little bit like you, is what I thought."

Vito glanced at the photo again, obviously intrigued, but didn't reply.

He sipped his wine. I drank mine, too, although in much smaller sips.

~

Several minutes later, after we talked about this book and another, Vito said, "You know …"

"Hmmm?"

"Some people in this neighbourhood think your husband is an undercover policeman."

My eyes popped wide open. I looked from him to Loretta, whose eyes were also wide open. Not in surprise at this revelation but in surprise that her husband had the nerve to confront me with it.

"They think what?" I asked Vito, alarmed but laughing,

because, honestly, I didn't know how to react to this shocking bit of news.

"It doesn't matter to us what your husband does," Loretta rushed in to reassure me. "We don't care."

"They think Hamlin is *what?*" I asked Vito again.

"They say he's a cop – an undercover cop."

"But why?"

"I don't know. But they're sure of it."

"He's not a cop, Vito and Loretta. Hamlin's not a cop." Neither of them spoke.

"You know us better than most people here," I said. "What do you tell them when they say that?"

"That if they have nothing to hide, they shouldn't have anything to worry about," Vito said.

"Vito, that's as good as confirming that he's a cop! Why didn't you just tell them it's not true?"

"But I don't know what your husband does for a living. It's not our business to ask. All I know is that you're nice people. You treat me with respect. You're friendly. You listen to my stories, you keep your place in good condition, you're nice people. That's good enough for me. I don't care if Hamlin is a cop."

"Ugghhh … What reasons do they give?"

"I can't remember anything specific. Maybe just that he looks like a cop."

"My poor husband. That's a new one."

Looking from Vito to Loretta, I said, "Do you want to know what Hamlin does?"

Vito shook his head. "I don't care. It's his business."

"It really doesn't matter to us," Loretta added.

That clinched it. They were trying too hard to reassure me. I needed to clear this up.

"He's a management consultant. He works with companies going through change. Significant change."

"So he doesn't work for the police?" Loretta asked.

"He did, but not the way you think."

Both their heads jerked up.

"He was on the police services board."

Their eyes fastened on mine. The house was so quiet, I heard a car horn beep in the distance. I realized I had made things worse.

"Do you know exactly what the police services board does?" I finally asked.

Loretta shook her head.

"It's a small board – about seven individuals – appointed by the province and the city. They are civilians – members of the community. Their job is to oversee the police, not be part of the police. Hamlin served two terms – six years. And then finished up and left."

"Well, I don't care what he does," Vito said again, ending the discussion.

I started to laugh and couldn't stop. Vito grinned. Loretta grinned. But I still didn't know if they believed me.

~

"You'll never believe what some of the neighbours think you do for a living," I said to Hamlin that evening.

"What do they think?"

"That you're an undercover cop."

His eyes widened with shock. "Why on earth would they think that? And where did you get this from?"

"Vito ... of all people. Vito, my friend. He said some people have told him they're convinced of it."

"What did Vito say?"

"Well, in all these years the topic of what you do has never come up. Mostly we talk about books, wine, gardening, his life ... and the times I worked in Italy. He tries to resurrect my Italian-language skills ..."

"So are you telling me Vito believes this? Vito?"

"I'm not sure whether he believes it or is just keeping his options open. He and Loretta like us, but the truth is, they don't really know what you do for a living."

Hamlin burst out laughing. "Imagine: we've lived here for years, and all this time my neighbours thought I was an undercover cop?"

"Not all our neighbours. A few. Well, maybe you have to look at it the way they do. To them, we may appear somewhat mysterious."

"Us? Mysterious?"

"Kinda. We're not Italian or Greek. We live in the old farmhouse of the area. Our property is tucked away behind these trees and shrubs. We have a huge fence, with sturdy gates. And very tall, thick trees. We obviously value privacy ... Maybe people think we have something to hide."

I continued musing. "For the longest time, because of my injuries, I rarely left the house. You were the one walking our dog, who was an enormous Akita. Some people, not knowing Kinu, assumed he was a ferocious dog. Imagine the picture you must have made: an athletic-looking black man walking a huge, fierce dog."

"Oh, come off it."

"Why don't we just go ask the neighbours? See what they think. Let them know you're not a cop."

"That would just give credence to the rumour. If they hadn't heard it already, now they'd be hearing it – from us."

We let the topic drop.

"Oh, darn!" I said, some minutes later.

"What?"

"The driver."

"What driver?"

"The driver from the police services board. He

regularly dropped off confidential police board docu-
ments for you to read. He drove a dark, unmarked car."

"Yes, of course. He was a member of the police
services, but he was always dressed in plain clothes."

"A plain clothes guy who looked just like a cop. And
he wore that long black cloth coat policemen sometimes
wear, like in the movies."

"Oh, Cynthia, come on. That's the movies."

"You don't think our neighbours watch the movies?
Like you and me and everyone else?"

"Ughhhhh ..."

~

Months later, one of my friends invited us to dinner. It
was rare for us to say yes to such invitations; we would
go only if I felt able to handle it. But this was one of my
closest friends, and she had invited guests both of us
knew and liked.

At the dinner, one of them, a Jamaican-born woman,
said she had read my book and liked the good relations
my family enjoyed with our mainly Italian and Greek
neighbours.

"Hamlin and I always seem to get along really well
with people from Southern Italy," I said.

"There are a lot of similarities between them and
Jamaicans, I think," said another woman, whose husband
was Italian. "They love family, they love to eat, they talk
and laugh loudly, they are religious people ... the list goes
on."

"There's only one problem," I said, laughing. "Seems
a few of our neighbours think Hamlin's an undercover
cop."

That got a good laugh.

"Seriously. They do. One of our other neighbours
told us."

"Well, let's see …" said Salvatore, the man sitting to my right. "Do they bring you gifts?"

"Yes. From their garden. Or stuff they've baked or cooked."

"That's a sign, right there," Sal noted calmly.

I couldn't tell whether he was genuinely concerned or stifling a smile.

"And wine. I get lots of wine," added Hamlin.

"Wine," Sal said nodding. "That's another sign."

A sign of what? I wondered.

"So let's think about this," Sal continued. "They're giving you vegetables and fruits, and cooked food. And wine; they're giving you bottles of wine …"

"Well, not everyone gives me bottles of wine," Hamlin explained. "Sometimes they invite me to their homes to taste the wine. Sometimes, after all the wine I've tasted, I can barely make my way back home. Those guys make very strong wine. It hits you before you know it."

"I know exactly what you mean," Sal said. "They're not only trying to be very nice to you by bringing all those gifts. They're also trying to get you drunk to see what you'll reveal."

"And how exactly do you know all this?" I asked.

"I'm Italian."

"But it all started when Hamlin helped out a neighbour whose snowblower broke down," I said. "He gave us food, just as a way of saying thanks. Then another neighbour's lawnmower broke down. Hamlin lent him ours. And that neighbour brought food. It's just the way it works in our neighbourhood."

I felt the need to defend my neighbours from these stereotypes. But Sal didn't let up.

"I see," he said. "Hamlin made the first move each time, by being helpful to the neighbours."

"Yes, but that's just the way he is, wherever we've lived."

"But they don't know that. They think he was just trying to get close, to find out things about them. We Sicilians know how these things work with you under-cover cops ..."

"My husband is not an undercover cop," I said. "And most of my neighbours are not Sicilians, and even if they were ..."

I stopped, noticing for the first time a suspicious twinkle in Sal's eyes. His mouth twitched. He quickly looked away. He was trying his best to suppress ... laughter. Sal, our Sicilian friend, had been pulling my leg. And I, in all my gullibility, had played the perfect straight man.

"Oh, my gosh!" I burst out. "You wretch, Sal!"

Everyone burst into laughter now, the kind that brings tears to one's eyes. Even I was laughing a deep belly laugh at how I'd allowed myself to be strung along by his performance.

But there was still the matter of what our own neigh-bours thought.

~

Every so often, as we drove home that night, we laughed.

"If Vito believes us," I told Hamlin between giggles, "I think we're okay."

"Vito? Vito is probably enjoying this completely. He's not going to correct them. He loves the intrigue. He loves telling our neighbours: 'If you have nothing to hide, you have nothing to worry about.'"

He did a surprisingly good impression of Vito.

"For all I know, Vito was probably pulling my leg, too," I said. "Just like Sal. I've not just lost my memory; I think I've lost my common sense, too."

It was marvellous to be chatting and laughing like a normal person about people we cared for. Our neighbours, our kind neighbours. So what if a few of them thought Hamlin was a police officer?

As we turned onto our street, Hamlin quietly said, "Well, at least the neighbourhood is safe. After all, we have an undercover cop living here."

We looked at our neighbours' homes and back at each other and exploded into laughter again.

"My husband, the undercover cop," I said as we entered our home. "How very exciting."

Chapter Forty

Hamlin's Perfect Birthday

Hamlin's birthday, in early July, was on the horizon.

Nikisha and Tim had decided to come home so the whole family could celebrate it. We wanted to do something small but special for the person who had held the fort over these difficult years. But what?

~

"My cup runneth over."

It's a line from one of our favourites: the twenty-third psalm, and it perfectly describes the rush of joy Hamlin and I felt when our children – including our son-in-law, Tim – were all at home with us.

I looked at my husband's face as we sat on the verandah together one afternoon, and the words came to my mind in an instant: his cup was running over with joy.

The joy of having us all under one roof; of being able to share a hug as we encountered one another in a room. The blessing of knowing the children were healthy and well and at home with us. It was the biggest birthday present anyone could give either of us.

~

"Joy," wrote Marianne Williamson, "is what happens to us when we allow ourselves to recognize how good things really are."

Indeed. Whenever I saw Hamlin looking at Nikisha, Lauren, and Tim, I could tell: his heart was so filled with joy you could feel it radiating from him.

~

Nikisha and Tim planned to take us all to dinner. They had emailed us from Seattle to see if we had a favourite restaurant nearby.

We didn't. So they picked one from the Internet.

On the evening of Hamlin's birthday, we dressed up and drove to the restaurant on a busy road in Markham, a city northeast of Toronto. I had noticed it before, but never been inside. The building looked more like a house than a restaurant.

We were greeted warmly and taken to our seats. Going to a restaurant was such a rare experience for me, I felt like a child all dressed up to have dinner with the grown-ups.

Hamlin beamed contentedly.

The waiters were dressed in formal suits, white shirts, and ties. In fact, the word "waiter" seemed inappropriate, even impolite, in this place. "Host" was more like it.

I looked around at the formally set tables, at the other diners, and at the hosts as they went about making everyone feel welcome, comfortable, and well fed.

And then I saw a familiar face.

"Hamlin!" I whispered. "That's George! This is George's restaurant!"

I dimly remembered our neighbour Kikki telling me once that her husband worked in a restaurant.

"George who?"

"George, our neighbour!"

We were both staring at the well-dressed man in the

middle of the restaurant when he looked up at us and smiled.

"How is it possible," Tim and Nikisha remarked from time to time, "that of all the restaurants in this region, we chose the one where your next-door neighbour works?"

"And chosen from the Internet!" Hamlin added.

George greeted us like long-lost family. He introduced us to his friend, the proprietor of the restaurant. Both of Greek origin, these two had known each other for decades and had worked together almost as long.

In honour of the occasion, George returned with a gift: a fine bottle of red wine. The owner of the restaurant also came to our table and regaled us with stories about famous people who had eaten at his restaurant.

The aroma of the food, the oft-repeated family tales, the gentle teasing, the frequent "happy birthdays" to Hamlin – it all made for one of the most heartfelt meals we had ever shared as a family.

Between the main course and dessert, I reached out and patted Hamlin's knee. He patted my hand and looked down at the table. His emotions were close to the surface. Moved beyond words, our eyes misted over as we looked at each member of our family.

As we turned in for bed that night, Hamlin said, softly: "It was the perfect birthday."

Indeed, it was.

My prayer that night was full of thanksgiving.

Our cup runneth over, I told God.

Chapter Forty-one

Sunshine and Clouds

For years, Hamlin was the rock I leaned on.

Without his enormous strength and stability, I would have simply rolled away until I was washed out to sea somewhere. Instead, he and our family had loved me back to life.

He was a strong man, a courageous man, a loving man.

I gave thanks for him every day and every night when I said my prayers.

In earlier years, I had been so distressed at my inability to help him, that I felt utterly useless. Guilt-ridden over the suffering I had caused him and our daughters, at the enormous burden I posed. My life felt worthless. I lost the will to live.

Hamlin helped me find my way back.

One day, he told me, yet again, that I was his rock.

"Even in this state, when you're flying on one wing – or no wing at all – you are my strength," he had said. "You have to believe that."

He held me in his arms, willing me to believe. And I finally did.

Getting better wasn't just about regaining what I had

lost; it was also about helping my husband regain what he had lost.

My diminished independence had taken much away from him. Money was a huge problem, yes. But there were things he would have liked to do that he couldn't because of my injured body.

We used to love dancing. We hadn't danced in years.

We enjoyed travelling. Hamlin now travelled only on business, always alone.

Long walks in the woods together once gave us a special joy. They were now impossible.

I wanted to get better partly as a gift to Hamlin. It was one of the reasons I kept taking the anti-anxiety drugs even when they produced awful side effects and only minor positive effects. It felt like my last chance, and I was giving it the best effort possible.

In the meantime, I took over more of the cooking, and while I was not a great cook, Hamlin appreciated my efforts.

He wouldn't allow me to help with the gardening, except occasionally to move the water sprinkler from one garden bed to another.

But I could listen to him, love him, and tend to him in small ways. A cup of tea. A small vase of flowers on his desk or bedside table. A mid-afternoon snack when he worked at his home office.

I also developed a habit of making or buying him a small, inexpensive gift every two weeks or so.

~

Hamlin received an email from his friend Ray. He had written it from his hospital bed.

Ray had been battling a blood disorder and received a bone marrow transplant; he had seemed to be recovering.

Ray's latest letter described his condition in positive

terms. But as Hamlin read on, he learned that his friend had lost a lot of weight.

"Cynthia!" he called out to me. "Ray's in trouble."

"What's wrong?"

"He's lost too much weight too fast. A man in his condition can't afford to lose that much weight." Hamlin's voice was weighed down by deep anguish.

I hugged him.

"Don't be surprised if he … If he doesn't make it," Hamlin whispered, disconsolate.

"We have to pray," I said, holding his hands. "Right now. For health for Ray. And for strength and comfort for his family."

~

A few days later, Hamlin went cycling with his friend Daryl. I expected that he would breeze in afterwards, pleased to tell me how far and well they had ridden together.

We the wives of the Freedom Riders – the name they gave their group – had laughingly practiced our "oohs" and "ahhhs," having decided that's all we would need to say when our brave men proudly returned home from their rides.

But today was different. "I don't know what happened to me," Hamlin said, "but I bonked."

It was the expression the cycling buddies used to describe a sudden loss of strength while riding.

"You've probably just been overdoing it a bit," I said. "Maybe you need to rest up before going out again."

But resting up didn't help.

Hamlin was having a tough time breathing, especially at night. He was sent for test after test, with no diagnosis forthcoming.

Finally, as the days wore on, his family doctor prescribed an inhaler to help clear his airways and enable him to sleep. But we remained concerned. I stayed awake every night, watching my husband, making sure he was breathing. Sometimes, he would settle into steady sleep only to start choking.

I contacted our friend Rosemary, a doctor herself, who called her friend Herbie, a well-known medical internist. More tests were done.

~

We came home from church to the news that Ray had died that morning.

Days later, we attended the funeral along with roughly eight hundred other mourners. Ray had been a wealthy philanthropist, financier, and university chancellor.

But for Hamlin he had simply been a friend.

~

Joy and anxiety overlapped that summer, like clouds and sunshine together in the same sky, neither giving way to the other.

By the fall, those emotions would be so intertwined that we scarcely knew where one ended and the other began.

Earlier in the summer, before Hamlin took ill, I had given in to a fit of optimism and finally set dates for two radio interviews about A Good Home. Both had been scheduled then rescheduled, several times. But now that the interviews approached, I felt anxious. How could I talk about my book when I was so worried about my husband?

Meanwhile, the PTSD and chronic pain continued to haunt me. It was almost a relief that I had returned to fitful sleeping at night. PTSD always waited for me to fall into restful sleep before attacking.

~

As the dates of the interviews got closer, I reminded myself that I still had my author toolkit. Sarah, my therapist, was far away and we hadn't talked in weeks, but she had helped me create coping strategies, and they had worked.

Yet, as I lay awake late at night watching my husband breathe, there were times when I thought about what would go wrong when I was interviewed. The stuttering and choking. The crying. The awful silences.

"I'm cancelling the interviews," I finally told my sisters and close friends. "I can't do this. I'm going to make a fool of myself."

Everyone replied with a version of: "You have come so far since the accident; you've overcome so much. You can do this."

One of my editors said, "This is an opportunity most authors would give their eye-teeth to get. And you have it! You're going to be just fine."

Although no one told me I was being an idiot for thinking of cancelling the interviews, I knew. Deep down, where the truth dwells, where no amount of worry or hysteria can change the facts, I knew I was very lucky to be granted these interviews.

I didn't cancel.

~

Meanwhile, there was another bit of good news. My licence was not withdrawn, after all. My family doctor and Dr. Helen had revisited my chart and decided there was no good reason to have the matter reviewed.

My head injury had not become worse. My neck and left arm were improving. Both doctors knew I didn't drive in bad weather, rarely took highways, or drove at night. And, after all, I had never suffered a PTSD-related attack while driving whereas I experienced them routinely when being driven by anyone else.

Their decision was a great relief.

Months later, however, I made a shocking discovery: I had been driving with an expired licence for well over a year!

Panicked now, I went to the local branch of Service Ontario and waited in a long line, only to be told I would have to do a test at a different location.

When I finally found the place, I ended up ruining five application forms then having to line up three times. But at least I passed the only test required: the vision test.

Later that day, Nikisha telephoned from Seattle, laughing. "Is it true you've been driving without a licence all these years?"

"Not years, Nikisha! Just over a year."

"Moth-err!" she replied.

Lauren found the whole thing hilarious. "Here you are, always after me to take care of things before the due date and to obey the law, and you've been driving without a licence for all this time! That's just too funny, Mom."

I had to agree that it was, at least, ironic.

Unknown to all of us at the time, that licence would come in handy before long.

Chapter Forty-two

The Test of a Man

The old Yiddish saying – "you're only as happy as your saddest child" – was so true.

With one daughter happily married, I prayed that younger daughter Lauren would achieve her heart's ambition. That she would find a good man.

One day that summer, she called, brimming with happiness.

"I met a guy," she said. "And he's nice. Very nice."

"That's great news! Tell me more. What's he like?"

"Well ..."

As she described him, I prayed that she had found the man of her dreams.

One Saturday morning, she arrived at our house to drop off the dogs. She and her new boyfriend were driving to his hometown, to the east of us. She had called ahead and warned me: "Mom, make sure you wear some decent clothes and get out of that old robe you normally wear. And comb your hair, please!"

I didn't argue. Sleeplessness had reduced me to a ragged mess. And if she could have seen me through the phone, she would have noticed that I was indeed wearing the old ivory-coloured robe, and that my hair was a mess.

So I changed into casual but "decent" clothes, combed my hair, put on some lipstick, and prepared a plate of fruit and pastry.

"This guy must really matter to her," I told Hamlin. "She wants to make sure we're presentable!"

His name was Dan. He was a bit nervous. I could tell because he gave long answers to whatever we asked him. But there was something likeable about him, and there was no mistaking the admiration and affection when he and Lauren looked at each other.

~

The test of a man is in what he does when you fall ill. My own experience had taught me that.

Within weeks, Lauren had caught a virulent flu which made her weak and, in her own words, "awful to look at."

She told Dan to stay away.

To her surprise, and ours, Dan refused. Instead, he looked after her, day and night. When we told Hamlin's mother about this, she said, "That's a good sign. He took care of her. He didn't leave."

The one day Dan had to leave – to take part in a rehearsal for a close friend's wedding – he went. But first he apologized to Lauren and us.

Hamlin's mother was right. It was a good sign.

Chapter Forty-three

Tea with Shelagh

The interviews came and went. I used my full toolkit for the first one, even finding moments to laugh.

The second one was more difficult. The interviewer came to my home, the place where I am most myself, and most vulnerable. By the time it was over, I couldn't remember most of what had happened. I knew I had cried and thought I had struggled with speaking at times. But little else.

My friend Marilyn had decided to be nearby. "Everything goes better with a cup of tea," she declared as she walked into the kitchen.

She prepared afternoon tea, using our mismatched but pretty china cups. We chomped on the scones she had freshly baked, dabbed them with clotted cream and fruit preserves, and munched on smoked salmon while Marilyn regaled us with tales about tea and tea paraphernalia.

It was a lovely afternoon.

Hamlin came out to the verandah to say hello to the group – Marilyn, Jacqueline the CBC Radio producer, Erin the sound technician, and Shelagh Rogers, one of the national broadcaster's most celebrated interviewers.

We were all grown women, and Shelagh was a celebrity

interviewer, but Hamlin looked at our happy faces and told us, "You look like a bunch of girls, giggling merrily!"

To that, we giggled some more.

~

I would hear the interviews myself along with hundreds of thousands of other Canadians that fall.

The first one surprised me: I sounded strong. My reading and answers were fluent. The interviewers were caring and skilled.

The second one made me cry. I found myself reliving the painful moments the interview described. But I was also thankful for the kindness of Shelagh Rogers and her team.

And, if you didn't know differently, you would have thought my sniffles were caused by allergies. It was a deeply emotional conversation, but the team had managed to maintain its honesty without damaging my dignity.

Chapter Forty-four

Hamlin's Sudden Turn

Yet another of my book-related events had been delayed, but, as my mother used to say, "Nothing happens before the time."

So there I was a few Sundays after the interview and afternoon tea, the guest of a Toronto book club and enjoying every moment of it.

Book clubs were my favourite groups. I had missed these visits in the months after my health relapsed.

My first visit with a book club had taken place a year earlier. Since then, I had learned to expect a warm welcome, genuine curiosity, and insightful questions and remarks from the members. Plus, the groups had great names like The Limberlost Club and The Ladies Literary Liquid Lunch.

It helped that each meeting of the club was held in someone's home. And that the participants were women who were not afraid to discuss the raw emotions the book evoked and the insights it offered and were quick to laugh at the hilarious parts of the book.

And it helped that I always had my author's toolkit to put into play.

The women this Sunday presented me with a gift and

a card of thanks and wished me a pleasant goodbye. I started on my way home.

I was approaching the turn-off to our home when I phoned to check in with Hamlin.

"Hey, you!" I said. "How's it going?"

"Great! I just finished the presentations I've been preparing. How did it go?"

"Really well. I love being with book clubs. But how are you feeling?"

"Great."

His voice over my hands-free phone speaker in the car sounded marvellously strong, his breathing normal. Just the day before, he had given the keynote speech at the national conference of Mothers Against Drunk Driving. The audience gave him a standing ovation. Back at home, he had shared the good news with me, and I had hugged him, grateful that his health had taken a turn for the better.

"Okay, then," I said happily. "I have to pick up something and then will be home soon."

～

The "something" was a small gift for Hamlin.

I either made or bought him a small gift about twice a month. The money came from book sales. I loved doing it. I loved the look of surprise on his face, especially when I had chosen well. And I loved the feeling that I finally had some money of my own that I could spend on him, for a change.

It always took me at least twenty minutes of trawling the aisles and peering at items on the shelves before I settled on a gift. It had to be something he would use, and it had to be inexpensive. So, since Hamlin loves to cook, I often headed to the housewares department of a nearby store to find something for under ten dollars.

He liked maple syrup on his pancakes, so I finally settled on a small bottle of it, but only after about a half hour of perusing the shelves.

~

Once I got home, I noticed that the side gate was open.

I walked into the house and placed Hamlin's wrapped gift on the kitchen counter. Beside it, I put my gift from the book club, which I decided we would open together.

I called out for Hamlin but got no response. I went upstairs to change my clothes, got distracted for some minutes then felt a sick sensation in my stomach.

Hamlin! I thought. Where's Hamlin?

The image of the open gate flew into my mind. In an instant, I was heading down the stairs.

"Cynthia! Help! Help me!"

The weakened voice belonged to my husband. As I reached the kitchen, I saw him lying on the floor. He must have crawled in after I went upstairs.

"The puffer ... the puffer."

I started to help him up from the floor. But he was asking me to get the inhaler his doctor had prescribed. It sat on the counter nearby, and was meant for emergencies like this one.

He took a hungry gulp from it, and I helped him sit up on the wooden floor and lean against the kitchen cabinet. His face was ashen and he was barely able to speak.

"Where were you?" he finally gasped.

"I just got home."

"But why didn't you come outside? I waited for you to come ... then I passed out again."

My stomach lurched. I had taken my own sweet time to choose a gift in the store. Once home, I had placed it just where he would see it when he came in and then had gone to freshen up.

And all that time, my husband lay unconscious on the ground in our garden.

~

I reached Herbie, the medical internist, at home.

"It sounds like an embolism," he said. "He needs to get to the hospital. Can you get him to Toronto Western?"

"Yes, of course."

Hamlin was barely able to sit on the low window seat in the kitchen. I frantically unlaced his gardening boots and removed them and rushed upstairs to fetch him a clean shirt. Then I was back down, helping him into it.

I helped him to my car. I put on his seatbelt.

Then I drove.

It's amazing what happens when you are trying to save the life of someone you love. You become calm enough to do exactly what must be done. And all the while, inside, your thoughts are a churning, boiling mess.

~

Eventually I would learn what had happened.

Hamlin had felt great after finishing up the two presentations he was to give over the next few days.

He looked out his office window and saw, once again, that the grass was getting tall. It would be harder to cut when he returned four days later. So he decided to cut the lawn and the boulevard outside our fence.

But his riding mower hit a tree stump and a belt came loose. It was when he climbed down from the tractor and yanked the belt back into place that he first passed out.

He regained consciousness long enough to drive the tractor through the open gate and into the back garden. But, as he stepped down from the tractor, he lost consciousness again, coming to just long enough to walk and crawl to the kitchen.

It was all too strange. Hamlin had always been athletic, and almost always healthy. I often accused him of being "aggravatingly healthy."

"Your body," I once told him, laughing, "is a temple to good health. Mine is a toxic dump."

In the years since the car accident, as I struggled with a host of injuries – including cracked teeth that left me eating soft and sometimes unhealthy food – Hamlin became even more disciplined about his fitness and diet. His body was trim, fit and strong.

A former 400-metre hurdles champion who represented Canada at international meets, he now cycled in the mild-weather months and cross-country skied as soon as there was enough snow.

"I have to be healthy," he replied to my frequent teasing. "I hate going to hospitals."

Athleticism and fitness had been part of his life for decades, and his yearly check-ups attested to his great health.

〜

But now we were on the way to the hospital's emergency department, and Hamlin was fretting aloud that he wouldn't make it.

He asked me to tell our daughters how much he loved them.

He said he was sorry he wouldn't be around to walk Lauren down the aisle on her wedding day.

And every so often, he gave me an instruction for his funeral.

〜

I was terrified. But I had to be calm – and not just because I was driving a car along busy Toronto roads. I needed him to stay with me, to keep hoping, to hang on until we reached the hospital and the doctors.

He faded in and out. In the moments when he was alert, he told me he loved me. And then he issued more instructions for his funeral.

"No open casket! No long speeches!"

"And no talking about death!" I finally said. "You are not going to die. I will get you to the hospital, and the doctors and nurses will make sure you live!"

I patted his hand and prayed.

That he would live.

And that I would have the strength to face whatever happened.

Breathe, I told myself and him. Just breathe.

~

I concentrated on getting through the traffic, the green lights, closing the distance between our home and the hospital.

I heard Hamlin say, "No one ever emerges from Emerg!"

Incredulous, I replied, "Most people do emerge from Emerg!"

Then I looked at him again to see if this was meant to be a joke.

It was not.

"Rest," I said. "Don't talk. Just breathe."

I kept driving.

~

From the moment we arrived at Emergency, Hamlin received the kind of care one prays for. The hospital staff took over. All, especially the nurses and the doctors assigned to his care, were kind.

Even the nurse who chastised me after hearing I had

driven Hamlin instead of calling an ambulance, did so gently.

We discovered later that Herbie thought we lived closer to the hospital where he worked. He had not known that it would take me forty-five minutes to get there.

～

When the news came, it was frightening.

Hamlin had suffered a pulmonary embolism. The doctors believed that the blood clot had formed in his thigh then eventually travelled to his lungs. Which explained why he had trouble breathing.

His heart had kept bravely pumping blood to his increasingly clogged lungs.

The doctors were astonished that Hamlin had survived. They seemed equally surprised this had happened to someone so fit and healthy. They searched for an answer to the mystery.

Meanwhile they put him on blood thinners to prevent further clots from forming. An intravenous tube ran from a plastic bag to his arm. Wires ran from his body to a monitor on a table behind his bed.

Lauren and I watched anxiously, trying to determine what the hills and valleys of the monitor's green lines meant. We jumped every time the monitor beeped.

Only later we would learn that athletes, including cyclists, were showing up in increasing numbers at thrombosis clinics. When we searched the Internet, we found story after story from athletes who had also experienced blood clots, some of which might have been caused by dehydration or over-exertion.

But none as massive as Hamlin's, it seemed.

～

My husband was alive. He had survived an attack that

would have killed most people. I was grateful and in my thankfulness, I felt hope.

It's not that I wasn't scared: in some moments I was terrified. But I couldn't afford to show fear. I did not cry. Whenever fear or uncertainty hit, I stopped and prayed silently. I had learned to pray in such moments.

Prayer, I had come to see, was an act of trust and humility: an acknowledgement that some problems were bigger than myself, bigger than my capacity to solve. Through prayer, I reached out to a bigger power and asked for strength for Hamlin. Next, I prayed for the strength and wisdom to handle whatever challenges were sent my way.

The very act of praying made me feel stronger – perhaps proving that the Danish philosopher Soren Kierkegaard was right when he said: "The function of prayer is not to influence God, but rather to change the nature of the one who prays."

I needed to be strong. I needed to demonstrate my certainty about Hamlin's survival. To his mother and sisters, to Nikisha and Tim on the phone, to Lauren here beside us, to anxious family members and close friends.

~

Nikisha and Tim had left for Asia just days before Hamlin's collapse. They had decided to visit Japan and Bali to celebrate their wedding anniversary.

"Don't tell them!" Hamlin had pleaded as we waited in his room in Emergency for the test results to come back. "It will ruin their vacation."

I understood and even agreed. But younger daughter Lauren and her boyfriend Dan talked about it and said if they were the ones travelling, they would want to know. I agreed with them, as did Nikisha and Tim when they found out. Together, Hamlin, Lauren and I assured them that Hamlin was recovering and urged them to continue enjoying their vacation.

Hamlin had asked that we not break the news to his mother until the next morning. She'd been suffering from back pain, but there was more to his request. Hamlin is her only son, and the two are very close. He wanted to shield her from worry for as long as possible.

When I phoned her early the next morning, I spoke as calmly and positively as I could.

"My God!" she said. "How is he now? What do the doctors say?"

And then, assured that he was in excellent hands at the hospital, she did what mothers the world over have done for centuries. First she prayed. Then she started cooking for her son.

I swung by her house in north Toronto to collect her and the containers of food. Next we went to Lauren's apartment building in mid-Toronto, and the three of us set out for the hospital. Lauren answered Mom's questions, and the two of them said comforting things to each other as I drove.

I kept my eyes on the road and silently said a prayer of thanks. Over and over, I thanked God for saving Hamlin's life.

And then I gave thanks that I still had my licence and could drive.

~

Hamlin's mother loved her family so fiercely that if one of us got sick, she would either send us a homemade cure or instruct us by telephone on how to make the remedy. If our region got a heavy snowfall overnight, she would call bright and early the following morning to caution us. The warnings varied from gentle concern to stern orders to her beloved son.

"You just keep your backside inside the house today! I don't care what appointment you have. Cancel it and stay home. The radio is warning about black ice on the roads – and you know what that means!"

We saved that voicemail message and listened to it occasionally. It always made us smile.

But I didn't know how she would react when she saw Hamlin in his hospital bed. Yes, she was a retired nurse. But it was one thing to nurse others and quite another to see your only son in critical condition.

She took a deep breath before entering his room. Then, in a manner both tender and matter-of-fact, she held his hand and talked to him in a steady voice. Despite her own severe back pain at the time, she stayed by his side for hours, watching over him, loving him, praying for him, and cracking the occasional joke.

~

When MaryAnn, Hamlin's office manager, heard the news, her voice broke.

But in the days that followed, she took over the reins of Hamlin's consulting company. Her take-charge manner was impressive.

You never know what strength people possess, even if you know them well.

Hamlin's close friends, Bill and Kingsley, were clearly shocked and worried, but in every phone call and visit, they supported and encouraged Hamlin and our family.

Lauren, I could tell, was as frightened as I was, but she was determined to hide her fear. That meant always being at her father's bedside when I had to go home to pick up some item or other. It meant never crying in front of him. And it meant bringing him breakfast every day and, at lunch and dinnertime, warming up the food that either she or Mom had made for him.

On the third day, when her father started to regain his strength, he asked for his laptop.

"No, Dad," she said. "You can't work. You're seriously ill."

When he said he felt guilty for cancelling the two presentations, she firmly reminded him it was not his fault and changed the subject to something more cheerful.

~

"God moves in mysterious ways," my mother used to say when events were too puzzling to be explained away as coincidence.

That Sunday afternoon, as he was cutting the grass, Hamlin had been planning to leave for the airport within hours to fly to Montgomery, Alabama, to make two speeches to business leaders over two days.

"Can you imagine if he had collapsed on the plane?" Lauren wondered aloud. "Or in Alabama, far from his doctors and family?"

And I wondered what would have happened if I had been at home to prevent Hamlin from getting on that mower, which I surely would have. It would have made the collapse in a foreign city, or on the plane, all the more likely.

~

Every night, I lay on a chair-bed in Hamlin's room. At first the contraption wouldn't recline. Since only one of my arms works well, I asked a nurse to assist.

"I'll help!" said a weak voice from the bed, from the man who was so used to rescuing me.

The nurse and I thanked him, smiled, and continued our efforts until we managed to turn the chair into a sort of bed. It was an odd-looking, uncomfortable thing, and I imagined even people who didn't have chronic pain would have been hard-pressed to fall asleep on it.

Awake for the whole night, I watched Hamlin breathe. When all the lights went out around us and I could no longer see, I occasionally got up and lay my hand on his chest, to feel him inhaling and exhaling.

And every time, I said a prayer of thanks.

~

We returned home several days later.

Hamlin was improving, but the ride exhausted him.

"Time to rest," I said cheerfully.

He complained – half-heartedly – about my sudden bossiness.

"Probably the only time I'll get to do it," I said.

He rolled his eyes and said something our daughters used to say when they were small and we had just instructed them to do something they didn't like, such as eat their vegetables.

"You're not the boss of me!" he said. But he was smiling.

Chapter Forty-five

Hamlin's Comeback

Things were different now.

I had always hated having to discuss my car accident. I hated having to acknowledge the pain and terror in which I lived, the tightrope I walked every second of the day, the nightmares that plagued my sleep.

I was afraid I'd cry but was even more worried about the flashbacks and anxiety attacks such discussions would likely trigger.

Hamlin and I had made a pact early on: we would say very little about it. We kept the extent of my injuries private, shared only among close relatives and a few friends. Only they had been allowed to visit me during the long periods I spent in bed, the times when I couldn't move, hold on to a thought, or speak without stuttering.

Even at church, few people knew all that we suffered. We showed up when I felt able to handle the walking and sitting, and stayed home when I couldn't.

Now, however, it was time to be more open, time to ask for help.

Our small eight-thirty a.m. congregation had noticed Hamlin's absence the first time he missed church. Some teased me, saying, "I see Hamlin has gone riding on this fine Sunday morning!"

I had simply smiled back at first.

But as Hamlin's breathing problems got worse, I confided in Reverend Claire and a few close friends.

The next Sunday when I attended church alone, I noticed that someone had put Hamlin's name on the prayer list. It felt strange to see it there: it had always been my name on the list.

The following Sunday, someone wrote: "Hamlin and Cynthia." Jane, I guessed.

When I called to thank her, she simply said, "You both need prayers right now." She had expressed the same sentiment for me years before – when I had been the one in trouble.

And, so, the day after Hamlin's collapse, I sent a quick email to let everyone know what had happened. As I expected, the church members started praying even harder.

~

Linda Collins, the bishop for our region of the Anglican diocese, had written a story about *A Good Home* shortly after it was published. She described my intermittent struggles with faith, noting that in those moments my church community had held my faith for me.

Since that article was written, my faith – in God, and in the future and myself – had slowly become stronger. Now, faced with this huge test, I was comforted that my church members were once again holding faith – not because Hamlin and I couldn't, but because they knew we would be strengthened by their own.

~

In the days and weeks after Hamlin's sudden hospitalization, some friends and relatives asked us, "How much hardship can one family take?"

After the painful challenges our family had been through in recent years, they wondered, why should yet another bad thing happen to us?

We understood how our friends and relatives felt, and we loved them all the more for it.

We would have asked these questions ourselves, in earlier years.

I would have raged – and indeed, I did, after the car accident smashed my plans to smithereens, damaged my body and mind, and messed up our lives.

But not now. Instead, I was overwhelmingly grateful. Grateful for every good thing that happened to our family.

Little things like my husband's smile, our children's laughter.

And now the biggest thing: Hamlin had survived and was recovering.

~

A week after Hamlin left the hospital, we returned for a follow-up visit. We were both nervous, even scared, and neither of us bothered to hide it. What would the doctors tell us? What lay ahead?

The supervising doctor, the one who had led Hamlin's care while in the hospital, now showed us on her computer screen the images of the blood clots in his lungs when he was first brought to the emergency department.

They were so widespread, so big, the doctor said, that the average person would have died. My husband's extremely strong heart and body had helped keep him alive.

Hamlin listened quietly. I scribbled in my notebook,

sure that neither of us would remember what we were being told.

Slowly, softly, as if marvelling at it all, Hamlin shared with the two doctors and me how he felt when he lay on the ground, floating in and out of consciousness. Realizing that he might never describe this again, I scribbled quickly.

"Each time I took a breath, it was as if a giant hand pushed me underwater," he explained.

"I didn't see any white lights, and I didn't feel content to die. In fact, I was angry. I thought about how Cynthia would feel when she came looking for me and found me dead in the garden."

He paused to catch his breath, and you could have heard a pin drop.

"I knew she would never get over that. I think that's what gave me the strength to crawl to the kitchen door."

My throat constricted and I stopped writing for a moment. All I could do was stare at him.

Hamlin said he saw everything around him very clearly. Every blade of grass. Every leaf on nearby trees. He heard every sound. Time moved very slowly as he lay there alone, close to death.

The three of us listened to his story, hardly knowing what to say. It isn't often a person comes that close to death and comes back and tells you what it was like.

"You may remember more later on," the supervising doctor said. "You should make notes when you do. Write it down."

~

In the weeks that followed, Hamlin paid visit after visit to other doctors attending to his care.

One doctor came from around his desk to shake his hand. "You are the miracle man," he said.

Another was more blunt: "You are bloody lucky! You should go buy a lottery ticket."

This I will always remember: My husband came back. My husband came back.

I had once mused about winning the lottery after my doctor recommended I spend the cold winter months in a warm climate. But this – my husband's return to life – was better than that.

Much better.

~

If you live long enough, you come to realize that nothing in life is guaranteed.

Two other men shared the hospital room – one after the other – with my husband.

One had just retired and had been looking forward to enjoying life after work. Instead, he was diagnosed with stage 4 cancer throughout his body. There'd been no warning, his wife said. No signs.

The next man had suffered a terrible relapse after a quadruple bypass operation.

"This only happens to one percent of patients, and my husband is the one percent," his wife said, shaking her head.

And yet these women took the time to console our family, and to pray for us.

As we did for their families.

~

From my journal, October 2014:

Why do bad things happen to good people? Many books have tried to explain it.

But this I know: we're not entitled to a long life.
We're required only to make the best of the life we have.

We find ourselves facing unexpected events – some good, some bad.

The bad hurts like hell sometimes. It makes the good all the more precious.

It's important to take joy – total joy – in the good times; to not do so is to cheat ourselves, somehow.

To wait for happiness to arrive is a very silly thing; finding joy should be mandatory.

This I know.

~

Of course, I didn't know what lay ahead. There were more tests to come.

"But he is alive!" I said often.

There was such joy, such gratitude in those words: he is alive.

As we say at the closing of the early morning service in our tiny historic chapel at St. Thomas' Anglican: "Alleluia."

Chapter Forty-six

In This Together

Family and friends had helped in the early weeks after Hamlin came home.

On our first night home, Rosemary and Peter arrived with several containers of hot Chinese food. They had supported us throughout the ordeal, but now it was time for food.

My old friend Lucia, a professional chef, sent meal after meal. Jean and Bill brought a huge basket with roast chicken and other dishes. Pamela's cooking kept us fed for days.

Nikisha and Tim arranged for a housecleaner; Lauren and Dan visited often, helping in a variety of important ways; Jan and Don helped with the garden. Hamlin's mother made us a variety of dishes, including Jamaican food. My sister Pat and her husband Keith helped out in big ways and small.

Hamlin's closest male friends had been shaken that someone so healthy could come so close to dying. Childhood friend Tasso, who had recently recovered from a critical illness, visited one day, alternately reassuring Hamlin that he'd recover and making him laugh.

It was inspiring watching these men with their old

friend. Hamlin's collapse reminded them of their own mortality, yes, but right now it was time to put that aside and reassure him. The Freedom Riders – Hamlin's fellow cyclists Bill, Don, and Daryl – called or emailed every day; as Hamlin got stronger, I could hear the relief in their voices.

Other friends called or came to visit. Every visit, every gift, every phone call, was a blessing.

By the end of November, Hamlin was getting stronger, and breathing much more easily. He wasn't out of the woods; that would take a while yet.

~

My health, meanwhile, had gotten worse. The extreme pain had taken hold, and I was exhausted. I had spent too many nights awake with pain and my compulsion to watch Hamlin, to make sure he was breathing.

I was performing the role Hamlin had occupied for years. It was gruelling. Without even knowing it, I'd missed my appointments with both my specialist and family doctor, and hadn't been to physiotherapy in months.

Sometimes, Hamlin and I had to prop each other up just to walk from one room to the next.

"Is this what it feels like to be old?" he asked.

"Yes," I replied.

Chapter Forty-seven

The Things We Do Not Know

There are some things we hide from those we love because we fear talking about them will make us weak when we need to be strong.

And then there are things we keep to ourselves because we fear that to even acknowledge them will weaken someone we love.

In the aftermath of Hamlin's hospitalization, there were things I didn't talk about with our children and things they didn't talk about with me. None of us ever admitted how terrified we were he might die. We had to keep each other strong.

It was only after he was well on his way to recovery – when the wound of our fears was healing over – that we revealed how frightened we had been.

Talking about it was a good thing. An important thing. And it reminded me of all the times when I had down-played my own injuries, refusing to discuss them or the fears raging through my broken mind.

What had this done to my children?

~

In the middle of discussing something else on the phone with Lauren, about three months after Hamlin's return from the hospital, I suddenly blurted, "One of these days I would like to know how it felt to have a mother in such bad shape ... That is, if you don't mind talking about it."

"I don't mind," Lauren said. "I can talk about it right now."

I wasn't expecting this. I tried to delay the talk.

"I would like to talk about it, and I think I can be quite frank." Lauren's voice was firm.

I tried to slow her down. "This is very important, and I don't want to forget. Can you wait while I grab a pen and paper?"

Once I was back on the phone, Lauren said, "It made us a lot closer, Mom. And it made me realize you're human."

"Really?"

"Really. Before the accident, you were always ten steps above me. Everything you did was right. You were beautiful, smart, powerful. You were perfect."

I was speechless. I had never remembered a time when I felt even close to perfect, but my daughter had seen me in a different light.

"You were this superwoman," she was saying. "But after the accident, you were suddenly making mistakes. It made me realize you're not invincible. That when you fall, you hurt."

I gulped and said the most original thing I could think of. "Really?"

"It also made me appreciate life so much more, and it made me appreciate my family even more."

"But it must have been very frustrating at times, my love."

"Of course it was. You'd finally agree to go to the store with me, and before I knew it, you'd need to sit on a chair somewhere, or go lie down in the car. And you couldn't remember anything."

"I'm sorry."

"You don't need to be sorry. I'm sorry I didn't realize what was going on. You didn't have a bone sticking out, but you were very different after the accident. Some days it made me frustrated. Not at you but for you."

I was not prepared for what came next.

"For a long time, I felt like you and Dad had a secret, and I just was not let into the loop."

"I'm sorry, Lauren."

"It's okay. I knew something was very wrong, more than just your physical injuries. But you weren't telling me and Dad wasn't telling me and I felt mad and didn't understand. I didn't like it at all and had no one to talk to about it."

The words kept spilling out.

"One day when we were driving on the road, I asked you a question and you couldn't answer it and you just started yelling at me. You kept repeating the same thing over and over and yelling out loud. It scared me and I realized something was very wrong. I was confused, mad, and frustrated."

By now I was crying. I suddenly remembered the moment when Lauren handed me a book about under-standing Alzheimer's disease. Her friend's mother had developed the disease a few years after a car accident and Lauren feared some of my symptoms were similar.

"I am so very sorry, my love."

"I know now you couldn't explain and that you were frightened, too. It felt like a cruel trick, because no name was given to what you were going through."

"When did this change?"

"The day we went to the therapist. It broke my heart, Mom."

Nikisha and Tim had been out of town that day, but Lauren and Hamlin had gone with me to see Sarah. Until then all they knew was that I reluctantly went off to therapy every week and came home with reddened eyes and a blotchy face and then went to bed. Not wanting to venture back to the perilous terrain of those sessions, I had never shared their contents.

"Why did it break your heart, love?"

"The therapist showed us the drawing of the mountain that you had made. We saw all the things you feared, and how worrying about those things made you feel."

Lauren paused, and I waited, my throat tight, the tears hot in my eyes.

"It explained how you had been feeling for all this time. You were sharing these things with your therapist, but you were afraid we would think less of you if you told us. You were afraid you were letting us down."

I couldn't have talked if my life depended on it.

"You didn't deserve to feel that way, Mom." Her voice broke.

"I'm sorry, sweetheart. I'm sorry."

Lauren wasn't finished talking. She had been waiting for years to have this conversation.

"The day we met with Sarah, everything suddenly made sense. We could now understand your behaviours and we had a name for it."

"Several names, you mean," I tried to joke. "PTSD, head injury, chronic pain, and depression."

She revealed how angry she had been at the driver who had crashed into my car.

"She did this and she didn't even know the damage and hurt it caused. And you insisted that she shouldn't be told. I couldn't understand that and I argued with you. But you said it would have been as if I had hit someone with my car.

"You had found out she was eighteen – almost the same age as me at the time – and you kept saying you didn't want her to go through her whole life with this on her conscience. I didn't understand it for a long time, Mom. But I do now. I understand."

We were both weeping by now. I finally found my wits and asked her something that had been troubling me for a long time. "Lauren, did you ever feel disappointed in me – that I was no longer a superwoman?"

"Maybe at first when I was younger ... and you couldn't remember things or hang out with me. But not any more. In fact, from the day we went to the therapist, it's like a wall came down. I understood that this person was still my mom and I just had to get to know her. It was a new chapter of my mom."

She went on to say that it made us closer. "I know the pain and PTSD are horrible, Mom, and I'm sorry for it. But I'm glad for the trust we have."

My daughter sounded as if she had been dying to talk, but I had been afraid to ask. More disturbing, still, was that, when I finally found the nerve to approach older daughter Nikisha on this topic, her responses echoed Lauren's. And my responses sounded just as lame.

"I'm so sorry, my dear daughter," I kept repeating, feeling even more foolish this time around.

Chapter Forty-eight

Hamlin's Revelation

And then there was Hamlin.

He and I had rarely talked about the accident itself.

I had no memory of the actual event, but that wasn't the only reason for our silence. We were both afraid that forcing myself to try to remember would spell trouble. Medication seemed to be helping a little these days, but we knew that PTSD still hovered in the wings, and we did not want to provoke it.

And yet I sensed that something had been bothering Hamlin and that it was directly connected to the accident. How long had I known this?

Probably from just before *A Good Home* was published. Why else had I not mentioned in the book the fact that Hamlin had been in the car with me? That he had, in fact, been in the driver's seat as we stopped and waited for traffic to pause so we could make that left turn?

I must have sensed that he felt guilty. And I did not want to add to his worries. Bad enough that I was consumed with guilt for not healing fast enough, for all the extra responsibility I had piled on his shoulders by not being able to permanently return to work.

I also wanted him to speak about the accident only when he was ready to do so and I was ready to hear it.

～

"You should write about it from your own perspective," I said to him one day. "From the moment of the accident to now – how it feels to have lived through all this, and to have survived it."

Hamlin just grimaced. I let the matter drop.

But after the recent conversations with our daughters, I knew Hamlin and I needed to have this talk.

"Why do I sense that even thinking about the accident makes you very uncomfortable?" I asked one evening.

We were in the kitchen, making dinner together. He was washing something at the sink while I was cutting vegetables at the other end of the kitchen counter.

He didn't turn around. Nor did he answer for what felt like several minutes.

"Ever thought that maybe I have survivor guilt?" he said at last. He spoke softly, but the words sounded loud in the quiet kitchen.

"Why on earth would I think that?"

"Because I healed in about three months, but you were seriously injured."

"But why?" I repeated. "You didn't cause the accident. You tried to protect me by shouting a warning."

He was wearing the same casual clothes from when he'd left home that morning – slim-fitting jeans and a black turtleneck sweater.

"You are one sexy man!" I'd said when he came to kiss me goodbye. "Is that the turtleneck I gave you last Christmas?"

"Yes," he had replied, smiling.

"Huh! Should I worry when you leave the house looking so fabulous?"

"I think you should!" he had teased. It was one of those moments of love and laughter between two people who had come to know each other so well over the years.

We were not laughing now.

Hamlin dried his hands and moved nearer to me, still not meeting my eyes. My heart lurched.

"I don't talk about it," he said, finally looking at me. After a long pause, he added, "But I sometimes wish I had been swift enough to swerve to the right. Maybe then you wouldn't have been injured."

It had been a calm spring evening and we were returning home from seeing a movie. As usual, we had taken the rural highway. We had slowed to a full stop, waiting for oncoming traffic to ease so we could turn left. Behind us, traffic overtook our vehicle on the right and continued on its way. Except for one car that did not move into the right lane and did not stop.

"How could you have swerved into the right lane?" I asked Hamlin now. "That was the lane for passing traffic."

He didn't answer, just shook his head numbly.

"If you'd swerved to the right and if the driver had done what she should have done, she would have clobbered us …"

"Which she did, anyway …"

"But not because you did anything wrong!"

"You … you don't understand," he said, his voice tight. "I saw the car lights when the driver was at the top of the hill behind us. I knew the driver was going very fast. I should have gotten out of the way."

"You're saying you should have known she wasn't going to stop?"

"I ... I can't help it," he said. "I know I shouted a warning, but I should have known you would have braced, whereas I deliberately let my body go limp. I should have said nothing at all."

"But listen to me ... please listen to me, Hamlin," I pleaded, moving closer to him and looking up into his beloved face. "It seems pretty clear that I braced, but we don't know if it was because of what you said."

He remained silent.

"No, I don't remember the accident," I continued. "But I do remember watching the cars coming off the hill behind us, one by one. I could see them in the rear-view mirror on my side of the car. That's what I remember doing."

A new thought came to mind. "I saw several cars that drove up behind us as we waited to turn ... I must have seen that car, too. Maybe that's why I braced."

"Did you?" he asked. There was cautious hope in his voice.

I wanted to tell him yes. I wanted to say that it was the sight of the speeding car about to hit us that made me brace. But I couldn't. I had no memory of that car.

I stared at his face then beyond his face, trying to re-enter the dark past of that night. I was doing something I hadn't been brave enough to attempt in years: trying to remember the accident. Trying desperately to remember, so I could reassure my husband.

"I don't remember," I finally conceded. "I still can't remember anything."

I did the next best thing I could think of. Walked over to my beloved man and hugged him hard, hugged him tight, and held him for dear life, repeating the words he had told me over and over through these challenging years.

"You have absolutely nothing to feel guilty about," I said firmly. "Absolutely nothing."

And I hoped – as he must have hoped all those times – I hoped that he would believe me.

Chapter Forty-nine

Out with the Snow Warriors

Snow falls every winter in Canada.

Grass grows in the spring and summer.

Leaves fall in the autumn.

And here, on this property that we loved, it all happened in great quantities.

~

The second snowfall of the winter of 2014-2015 fell with a mighty thud, but Hamlin and I may have been the only ones who heard it.

The autumn leaves lay on the lawn where they had fallen, and several of the gardening chores remained undone. Neither of us had been able to handle them, and we had forgotten to ask for my brother's help.

But it was the heavy snow that fell over a night and a day that made the biggest noise in our hearts.

We were both wounded warriors. How would we get through the winter? Who would clear the snow today?

As I watched it pile up, I knew with certainty it would have to be me. The local snow removal companies were all busy. Hamlin was at a doctor's appointment; I would have to do it before he came home. Otherwise, the snow would be too thick for him to handle easily with the snowblower. His heart, weakened by the hard work it had required to keep him alive, was strained.

My right arm had become stronger over the years – it had been forced to – but my left arm, though improved, was still weak and given to sharp pain if I pushed it too much. The right side of my body, from my back to my foot, was still a mess.

There would be a price to be paid, and it would come in the form of horrible pain, but the alternative was unacceptable.

I pushed and shoved and cleared the two walkways to the house. Then I pushed and shoved and cleared half of the driveway. Enough for Hamlin to drive in and park the car.

Next door, Kikki and Diane were also clearing their driveways, and looking at them gave me extra strength.

～

Life, someone once said, is what happens when you're busy making other plans. I had not gone to my neighbours' homes for cooking lessons, though I had visited to apologize for changing the plan.

"Life went and changed on me," I said. "I'd never published a book before. I also had no idea I'd have to spend all those months in bed."

"Life is like that, Cynthia," Kikki had said.

"Oh, Cynthia," Diane said, forgetting to speak in French just this once. "We will do this another time."

"A la prochaine," I replied in French.

She nodded approvingly.

～

On the night of the first snowfall, it was Kikki who had cleared our driveway for us, knowing Hamlin and I were in no shape to do it.

The women in our neighbourhood were snow warriors, as I had once been. I had looked out my window and envied them on many a winter day over the years. Now, surprised to see me holding a shovel, they hollered a cheery greeting across their snow-covered lawns and driveways, and Diane gave a yell of approval at my efforts.

Perhaps it was the most neighbourly thing they did that day.

Neither woman chided me, or warned me to stop what I was doing.

At last I was a snow warrior, too. Wounded, barely standing straight at times, but at least pushing the snow from one spot to the next.

~

Where does strength come from? Where does determination – even the foolhardy kind– come from, the kind that keeps you going even when your body cries out for mercy?

I could not answer that question. I knew I was about to pay a hefty price. I also knew Hamlin and I couldn't continue in this way.

Chapter Fifty

Making Advent Count

The coming year would bring more changes, I knew. My mind and heart needed to be at peace. And my faith would need to be strong.

By Christmas, certain decisions would have to be made.

～

For practicing Christians, Advent, the four-week period before Christmas Day, marks the season of waiting for Jesus' arrival into the world. It is a time of spiritual preparation for Christmas.

I had never paid much attention to Advent except on the four Sundays before Christmas when we lit the Advent candles in church.

This year, I decided to make Advent count. Not just on Sundays but on the weekdays, too.

Each day, I did one thing to prepare for Christmas. And each day, I prayed.

I thanked God for my family. I gave prayers of thanks for my husband's life. I prayed for guidance and strength to help our family face the future. And then I did one thing to show my joy in the season.

Each day, I added a few more ornaments to the Christmas tree. Some I held in my palm for a long moment, soaking up the memories they evoked.

I lifted the Christmas stockings out of the box where we kept them during the year. Each had a label on it, and as I looked at each stocking, I smiled. The name of one family member was clearly written on each stocking.

Even Julius and Dawson, Lauren's dogs, had their own stockings. Before Christmas Day, we would stuff small bags of treats or a bone into each one.

I hung all of the stockings from a window ledge, each held in place by a heavy iron stocking-holder. Nikisha and Tim would not be home, but theirs hung there, too. To do otherwise was unthinkable.

Dan planned to spend Christmas Day with us this year.

"Can you please hang a stocking for Dan?" Lauren phoned to ask.

"Of course," I said, reaching for an unassigned stocking.

At the bottom of the box lay two others: Mama's, made from an elegant winter-white fabric, and Kinu's, made of thick, quilted red and green cotton.

Mama and Kinu were no longer with us, but I had kept their stockings in the box with the others, seeing no reason to get rid of them or even to reassign them.

Perhaps one day, but not just yet.

～

This Christmas would have to be different, I told myself. We were being even more frugal than usual. We would give only small and inexpensive gifts. And I would spend no money on Christmas decorations.

No big pot of poinsettia; no Christmas arrangements for our front door, unless I made them myself. We would use what we already had, or could make.

It had been that way in our family for several years now, but I had always felt a bit regretful about this forced frugality at Christmastime. If only I had an income, I'd think.

This year, I decided to abandon wishful thinking and, instead, take joy in our blessings. I would be especially thankful for family and home. I would be grateful that I could actually make some family gifts and home decorations with my own hands. And I promised myself I would pace my activities to prevent further pain and setbacks.

And so I wrapped the jars of jellies and jams I had made late that summer, and the amaryllis bulbs that had already formed their flower buds and would bloom just after Christmas.

Over one week, I made several Christmas arrangements and placed them in containers that flanked our front and side doors. Most of the ingredients came from our garden: spruce and pine branches; red twigs from dogwood shrubs; branches of boxwood and cedar; dried hydrangea flowers; pine cones. A few had been saved from arrangements sent to Hamlin after he came home from the hospital.

~

Hamlin and I had both grown up in homes where the "good" dishes and glasses were saved for "when the governor-general comes to visit." Of course, the governor-general never came, and the dishes stayed unused in the china cabinet.

One December day, I spread a "good" red tablecloth on the dining table then took the "good things" out of the cupboard and placed them on the table. I loved the scalloped edges of the Villeroy and Boch plates, including the salad dishes that bore a Christmas pattern.

Next, I set out our "good" silver-plated candlesticks.

Hamlin added festive napkins and drinking glasses edged with Christmas themes. To my chagrin, he replaced the white candles with red and green ones "to match the salad plates and the tablecloth."

He was so pleased with himself that I couldn't help smiling.

Chapter Fifty-one

A Quieter Christmas

Hamlin was recovering. We would be in church again this Christmas Eve.

We had been attending the Christmas Eve service from back when St. Thomas' Anglican was a tiny but well-known church. Now, with a big new sanctuary to accommodate a much larger congregation, the church was beautifully decorated each Christmas.

Even on rough days when standing and sitting were difficult for me, I insisted that we attend the Christmas Eve service in this village where we lived ten years earlier. We looked forward to the participation of the children, the stories about Jesus' birth, the Christmas sermon, the reading of the prayers, and – most of all – the Christmas carols.

Now, as we waited for the service to begin, I was struck by a memory of the season in my family church in Jamaica. I turned to Hamlin.

"Did you ever make up different words for Christmas carols?" I asked.

"Like what?"

"While Shepherds Washed Their Socks by Night ..." I sang under my breath.

"Of course. All kids do that."

"Oh! And there I was, thinking my siblings and I were oh-so-clever."

Lauren, Dan, and I had dressed for the occasion. It was, after all, the most special night of the year. We wore, if not our very best clothes, at least some of our best. Hamlin, meanwhile, looked elegant in a stylishly cut black suit, crisp white shirt, and a handsome tie.

Before we left home, I had teased him that he was putting special effort into choosing his clothes because he was reading the prayers. He almost always read the Bible lesson or prayers at this the second of three services held at St. Thomas' on Christmas Eve. I felt grateful and proud that he felt well enough to do so again this year.

I glanced at him now, seated to my right, and thought how distinguished he looked.

I opened the hymnbook and came across the afore-mentioned carol and nudged him with my elbow.

He looked at the open hymnbook.

"Bet you can't do that tonight!" I said.

He didn't even ask me what "that" was.

"I bet I can."

~

It was time.

The organ music started. With a great rustle, the congregation took to its feet.

I stole a glance at my good man. He looked very dignified. Then I heard him sing, clearly:

While shepherds washed their socks by night,
All seated on the ground,
The angel of the Lord came down
And passed the soap around …

I giggled – then joyfully joined him as we switched to the original version, which our family sang with all our hearts.

~

If there was ever a Christmas where we needed to pace ourselves, this was it.

I continued to keep an anxious eye on Hamlin and tried to moderate my own activities. His health had improved, but the last few months had worsened my pain and worn me down.

My right shoulder, the strong one, had been uncomfortable for months – a result of leveraging the cane to support my weak right side for years – but now it had become downright painful. Shovelling that snow had been a good but not smart thing to do.

We opted for a quiet Christmas Day again this year: just Hamlin and me, Lauren and Dan, and "the boys," Julius and Dawson. It was a day of quiet celebration, of gift sharing, of laughter.

Nikisha and Tim had been travelling a great deal in previous months and decided to stay in Seattle. We settled for a long phone call and occasionally hugged each other when one of us felt a pang of longing to have them here with us.

It was Dan's first Christmas with our family. Lauren expressed dismay that his stocking held more small gifts than hers.

"That's not fair!" she exclaimed in mock outrage.

"Your stocking fillers were too big for your stocking," we explained.

"Then you should have bought smaller ones. My stocking is empty!"

~

On Boxing Day, relatives arrived at our mudroom door two by two and the usual flurry began. Hugs, kisses, and the handing over of coats, gifts, and packages, all to the music of dogs barking.

While Lauren put away their coats, our visitors entered the kitchen where Dan was on "drinks duty" and Hamlin and I were putting the finishing touches to the meal.

There was no turkey this year. We were following our pledge of using what we had, and shopping very judiciously, and what we had in the freezer was a large leg of lamb and a filet of salmon. We added a small ham to the menu.

My sister Pat had made her usual macaroni and cheese pie – a family favourite – and her famous Christmas cake. She knew she had to contribute these two dishes to our Christmas gatherings or risk rebellion from the ranks.

We knew that Hamlin's mother – whom everyone called Mom – would likely bring two delicious Jamaican dishes: rice and peas and escovitched fish, seasoned with garlic, onions, peppers, pimento, and vinegar. And bring them she did, in large boxes and bags full of containers, along with a bottle of sorrel, the dark-red Jamaican Christmas drink.

As drinks were poured, our close friend Kingsley issued a warning: "You have to watch out for Mom's sorrel. That delicious flavour is deceiving. There's a lot of alcohol in it."

My brother Michael brought a bottle of wine, as did Kingsley.

Christmas dinner was splendid.

Hamlin's salmon and lamb dishes came in for high praise, as did Mom's Jamaican dishes.

I protested that no one had complimented me on the sweet potato dish. "And isn't it a shame that a person who tries so hard at cooking has to turn around and fish for compliments so desperately?" I asked.

Everyone laughed then hurried to assure me my contribution was delicious.

But the big favourite was Pat's Christmas cake. It was so popular that family members devised clever excuses to be left alone with it in the dining room.

Lauren quietly coerced Dan into asking me for a second helping of Christmas cake. She figured I wouldn't dare deny an extra slice to a guest, but Dan looked so uncomfortable making this request that the jig was up within seconds.

A special moment was when we called Nikisha and Tim and spoke to them on the speakerphone so everyone could hear their voices.

It was a lovely Christmas.

Chapter Fifty-two

Farewell to the Farmhouse

A decade ago, before the car accident, I would not have thought there could be anything good about being stuck in an old house.

I would have been horrified at the idea of being forced to slow down, to live on reduced income, to withdraw from many of the things I enjoyed.

Indeed, I had fought against it all after the accident, waging a silent war that threatened to corrode my very soul.

It had been a long journey from there to here. And now, as 2015 heaved into view, it was time to move yet again. Hamlin and I needed an easier place to live.

～

Not that Hamlin embraced the idea of moving. Something about the farmhouse and its grounds spoke to his spirit. I had often teased him that he was a farmer in a previous life, but I also knew that it was the solidity of the house, the sheer strength and integrity of it, that he connected with.

He had never loved a place as much as he loved his Ambercroft. He had loved it from the start.

It had taken me longer, but the farmhouse and I had also bonded powerfully. I felt the spirit of this place: this home that had sheltered and been loved by generations of dwellers with roots in far-flung places such as Scotland and, now, Jamaica.

We had lived our times, our seasons, our human emotions here within the shelter of these walls, under this roof, and on these grounds.

The daydreams and dashed dreams, the times of comfort and despair, times of hardship and moments of simple joy.

All happened here.

And always, love.

To live and love here – in the joyful springs and summers of this house, the memories that returned with its autumns, and the silent reckonings of its winters – was to understand the rhythms of being human.

Others had experienced these seasons before us, and others would after us. And the house, protected by a historical designation and by the sheer marvel of its construction, would survive.

But that didn't make the thought of leaving any easier. Not for Hamlin, not for our family, and not for me.

～

Whenever we thought we knew a lot about Ambercroft, we were in for more learning. Weeks after *A Good Home* had been sent to press, another visitor dropped in. Another descendant of the original family.

When he realized that Hamlin and I were both former employees of the Canadian Broadcasting Corporation, he shared surprising news: one of our predecessors in this home was the man who had started up programming for the radio broadcaster that became the CBC.

Ernest Austin Weir might not have come here if life hadn't changed on him some years earlier. Ernest had moved as fast as he could to provide the quantity and quality of Canadian radio programming that his bosses demanded. But it was deemed not fast enough, and he was forced to leave that auspicious role a year later.

Ernest and his wife were the first people outside the original family to own the property. It was while here that he researched and wrote much of the book that was to become the definitive history of the early years of Canadian broadcasting, an achievement that brought him national acclaim.

I had been a leader in Canadian broadcasting, at the national broadcaster that Ernest had helped to establish decades earlier. Hamlin had been a senior journalist, interviewer, and news presenter there. And to think we went so long not realizing we were living in a home that had once been loved by the great Ernest Austin Weir.

~

I smiled at stories from people who grew up in the farmhouse.

Margaret, on her first visit back to the house in many years, gazed at the staircase's gleaming brown maple handrail and said, "I don't think I ever walked down this staircase. I always slid down it."

"Which explains why it's so shiny and well polished," I said.

The look in her eyes said she'd like to do it again – even if just once – but she was a grown-up lady now.

~

And always, there was Bert, the tall, handsome, blue-eyed octogenarian whose return visits made him cry. His mother, father, and younger brother all died long ago; his visits reconnected him not just to his youth but also to them.

Hamlin and I were always ready to welcome him. He walked through each room, caressing the walls and doorways. Sometimes I reached out to pat his arm, and sometimes to give him a warm hug. He always hugged back.

He called me one night a few years ago, to say, "I keep wanting to tell you that, if my parents and grandparents were here, they would love you. You and your family – you're special people, you know. If my parents and grandparents were here, they'd thank you and Hamlin for taking such good care of our house ... And since they're not here to do it, I want to thank you."

I thanked him back, a big lump in my throat

~

Where would we go next?

We had no idea. We told our realtor that we needed a one-level house with a small garden. And maybe – just maybe – a stream? But when she occasionally sent us pictures of bungalows on acres of land, I saw the gleam in Hamlin's eye.

"That gleam better not turn into a flame!" I warned him. "Remember: a one-level house with a small garden. We can't handle a lot of land."

"What about the stream?" he said. "And mature trees. We need a few mature trees."

I rolled my eyes and sighed. It was unlikely that we would find a small place with all these attributes, but I decided that now was a good time to be quiet. After all, how much can you take away from a man who had gone through so much? Especially now, when he had come back from the brink?

But life has a way of surprising you.

When we least expected it – after weeks of searching and looking and many disappointments – we found a house.

It was a one-and-a-half-storey brick house with a finished basement. It was located east of Toronto, which would bring us closer to our church and the authors' group I had recently joined. Hamlin also noted, with a smile, that there were bike lanes on some of the local roads.

Unlike the farmhouse, it was a very plain structure from the outside. But this house had its merits. Kitchen, living room, and dining room – even a bedroom and bath – were conveniently situated on the main floor.

Like the farmhouse, this house had big windows, which was a blessing, for clearly visible from the back of the house was a big surprise: a stream meandering through mature trees.

A prayer answered.

"Go figure," Hamlin and I laughed, as we looped an arm around each other and faced our future together.

Acknowledgements

I may be the author of this book, but I've had supporters all around me. I thank them here.

My family: My husband and children. Siblings Yvonne, Pat, Jackie, and Michael and their families. Uncles Jack, Gerald, and Edward; mother-in-law Merle; brothers-in-law Sam and Keith; sisters-in-law Fay and Olivia; and cousin Norma. Bless you all.

It's tough supporting someone with complex injuries and/or PTSD, as families the world over know. This book pays tribute to my family and all such families.

My doctors: Dr. Helen, who pushed me to "write!" and still does. Dr. Gage, psychiatrist. Dr. Hooks, who has supported me throughout.

My therapists: These include therapists at Toronto Rehab and also Sarah Johnson. Sarah wrote the piece on the link between PTSD, pain, and depression at the back of this book; she also reviewed and fact checked the manuscript from a therapist's perspective.

My first readers: Lauren Reyes-Grange, Lisa Eracles, Dale Ratcliffe, Jean Gairdner, John Garside, Arna Sloan, Kamala-Jean Gopie, Gail Scala, Tim Knight, Jacqueline Denomme, Pia Marquard, Marilyn Mirabelli, Mandy

Henderson, Diane Taylor, Nikisha Reyes-Grange, Tim McCarthy, Dan Leca, and Hamlin Grange. Thanks also to editor and book reviewer Katherine Jackson, my last reader.

My editors, mentors, contributors: Lesley Marcovich and Don Bastian, for kind patience and great skill. Kamela-Jean Gopie, for the discussion guide. Stephanie MacKendrick, for the painting of Ambercroft on the cover. Edward Gajdel, for my author photo. Djanka Gajdel, for inspiring the title.

The Canada Council for the Arts: Your support was crucial.

And finally, my readers and blogging community; my email group, known as The Loopers; my writers' group. Your support matters.

About Post-Traumatic Stress Disorder

by Sarah Johnson, MSW, RSW

The following information is intended to provide a general overview of the conditions of post-traumatic stress disorder (PTSD), co-occurring depression, and/or chronic pain. If you think you may be affected by a mental health concern, consult your family doctor or another trusted health-care professional. The views or opinions expressed in any of the information offered here do not necessarily reflect the opinions of the author or people or organizations with whom the author is affiliated. The writer has no conflict of interest arising from mention of any of the references included.

Post-traumatic stress disorder was not formally designated a psychological disorder until the American Psychological Association included it in the Diagnostic and Statistical Manual, version 3 (DSM-3), in 1980. In the most recent version, DSM-5, published in 2013, PTSD is classified independently under Stress-Related Disorders.

Sarah Johnson is a mental health liaison worker for Fraser Health Authority, British Columbia. She received the Master of Social Work degree from the University of Toronto.

The Symptoms of PTSD

For individuals over the age of six to be diagnosed with PTSD, they must experience symptoms in the categories below for the duration of one month or more, based on exposure to an actual traumatic event, including: direct experience; witnessing an event occur to others; learning of a traumatic event occurring to someone close to them; repeated exposure or extreme exposure to circumstances related to traumatic events.

The symptoms must cause significant disruption and/or impairment in social, occupational, or other important areas of life, and the symptoms must not be attributable to substance use and/or physical health condition(s). Additionally, to be diagnosed with PTSD, there must be evidence of (1) psychological and/or emotional distress and (2) physical reactions in response to triggers reminding of the traumatic event.

The four categories of symptoms are:

1. Intrusion symptoms (re-experiencing), which remind of the traumatic event, specifically:
   a. Recurrent memories of event (flashbacks).
   b. Recurrent dreams of event (nightmares).
   c. Dissociative reactions to the memories or dreams where individuals feel that they are reliving the traumatic event, i.e., "de-personalization" – feeling outside one's body; or "de-realization" – unreality of surroundings, distant, distorted, or dreamlike experience of surroundings.

2. Avoidance behaviours in reaction to stimuli associated with the traumatic event, such as:
   a. Avoidance of distressing memories, thoughts, or feelings related to traumatic event (using distraction techniques).

b. Avoidance of external reminders (i.e., person, places, things) that trigger memories, thoughts, and/or feelings related to traumatic event.

3. Negative cognitive functioning and/or changes in mood since the traumatic event occurred; specifically, they:
   a. Are unable to remember aspects of the traumatic event.
   b. Have negative, flawed core self beliefs.
   c. Distort the cause of the event to facilitate self-blame or blame of others.
   d. Experience persisting emotional distress.
   e. Lack interest or engagement in previously enjoyed/important activities of daily living.
   f. Feel detached or estranged from others.
   g. Lack the ability to experience positive emotions.

4. Arousal symptoms, or physical hyper-reactivity in response to the traumatic event; specifically, they:
   a. Feel and/or act irritable.
   b. Behave recklessly, or exhibit self-destructiveness.
   c. Exhibit hyper-vigilance.
   d. Have a heightened startle response.
   e. Have difficulty concentrating.
   f. Experience disrupted sleep.

Sources for the above:

Desk Reference to the Diagnostic Criteria from DSM-5. American Psychological Association, 2013.

Levin, A. P., Kleinman, S. B., & Adler, J. (2014). DSM-5 and Posttraumatic Stress Disorder. *Journal of American Academy of Psychiatry Law* 42: 146-58.

Koch, W. J. (2002). Post-traumatic Stress Disorder and Pain Following Motor Vehicle Collisions.*British Columbia Medical Journal* 44(6): 298-302.

The Impact of PTSD

The implications of living with post-traumatic stress disorder can spread beyond affected individuals to their family and psychosocial networks. Potential impact includes co-occurring mood disorders such as depression and chronic pain. Beck & Coffey (2007) found that approximately half of people with PTSD suffer from a concurrent mood disorder. They also found that chronic pain related to a motor-vehicle accident was a significant co-occurring condition specifically for individuals with MVA-related PTSD.

Individuals with PTSD may experience co-occurring substance misuse or other addictive coping behaviour(s); increased suicidal tendencies (ideation, attempts, death); damaged relationships (often a result in personality changes that occur post-trauma, such as irritability and social isolation; social isolation; a noticeable decrease in psychosocial functioning, e.g., in their involvement in previously enjoyed activities, occupational roles, relational roles).

Sources for the above:

Koch (2002), *op. cit.*

Palyo, S. A. & Beck, G. (2005). Post-traumatic Stress Disorder Symptoms, Pain, and Perceived Life Control: Associations with Psychosocial and Physical Functioning. *Pain* 117(1-2): 121-27.

Beck, J. G. & Coffey, S. (2007). Assessment and Treatment of PTSD After a Motor Vehicle Collision: Empirical Findings and Clinical Observations. *Professional Psychology: Research and Practice* 38(6): 629-39.

Common Co-occurring Conditions with PTSD: Depression and Pain

Depression

Depression (mild/moderate/severe depressive disorder) occurs in about 10 to 20 percent of the population. The chance that an individual diagnosed with PTSD will develop depression is 3 to 5 times more likely than in the general population (Kessler et al., 1995). Depression can occur organically, meaning it comes on for no apparent reason, or it may occur following a traumatic event, such as a motor vehicle accident, or significant stressful life change, such as chronic pain subsequent to the accident. Situational depression can develop for individuals following traumatic events. This can be either related to the distress around the event itself or to the individual's loss of functioning and/or resulting loss of sense of self.

For individuals to be diagnosed with depression, they must experience the following symptoms lasting most days for duration of at least two weeks: a loss of interest in things previously enjoyed; disrupted sleep, i.e., difficultly falling or staying asleep; increased or decreased appetite; feeling down, sad, or hopeless most days; having difficulty concentrating; have increased social isolation behaviour; and potentially feeling like hurting oneself (more common in severe depression).

Many symptoms of depression overlap with symptoms of PTSD (e.g., disinterest in previously enjoyed activities, social isolation, irritability, disruption to sleep, low mood, emotional numbness, feelings of loss of control). Shih et al. (2010) found that about one-third of those who have experienced a physical trauma will develop PTSD and/or depression. They emphasize early prevention and screening for a trauma history and subsequently, symptoms of PTSD and depression, to decrease the impact of the traumatic incident on functioning.

Mild to moderate depression is most often treated with counselling or other therapy; more severe depression is treated as well with medications. Some treatments of PTSD are effective treatments for depression, e.g., Cognitive Behavioural Therapy (CBT).

Sources for the above:

Centre for Addiction and Mental Health website.

US Department of Veterans Affairs National Center for PTSD website.

Shih, R. A., Schell, T. L., Hambarsoomian, K., Marshall, G. N., & Belzberg, H. (2010). Prevalence of PTSD and Major Depression Following Trauma-Center Hospitalization. *Journal of Trauma* 69(6).

Kessler, R. C., Sonnega, A., Bromet, E., Hughes, M., & Nelson, C. B. (1995). Posttraumatic Stress Disorder in the National Comorbidity Survey. *Archives of General Psychiatry* 52(12): 1048-60.

Pain

The experience of chronic, persistent pain frequently occurs in those diagnosed with PTSD, particularly for trauma survivors of a motor-vehicle accident (MVA).

Pain can actually exacerbate PTSD, as it can be a physical reminder of the traumatic event.

A diagnosis of PTSD and having co-occurring pain symptoms following motor vehicle accident are associated with diminished psychosocial functioning such as in social interactions, emotional regulation, and ability to communicate. Additionally, having symptoms of pain and a diagnosis of PTSD are associated with the individual's perception of decreased life control. Palyo & Beck (2005) found that diminished perception of life control is also associated with greater psychosocial impairment. Duckworth & Iezzi (2005) determined that individuals with chronic pain and PTSD symptoms have greater rates of physical impairment, negative cognition and mood and poor strategies for coping with pain.

Beck and Coffey (2007) discuss how, in the treatment of co-occurring PTSD and pain, individuals may experience difficulty in discerning symptoms of pain versus PTSD. Learning to discern the differences can be an important aspect in the survivor's therapeutic process, including instilling coping skills to work through the negative cognitions that have resulted since the trauma took place and/or how the pain has impacted their functioning.

Sources for the above:

Beck & Coffey. (2007), *op. cit.*

Koch (2002), *op. cit.*

Palyo. & Beck (2005), *op. cit.*

Duckworth, M. P. & Iezzi, T. (2005). Chronic Pain and Posttraumatic Stress Symptoms in Litigating Motor Vehicle Accident Victims. *Clinical Journal of Pain* 21: 251-61.

Management and Treatment of PTSD and Co-occurring Conditions

Treatment for PTSD can be of short-term duration (within six months) or longer – sometimes several years. The duration of symptoms of PTSD can depend on early detection through screening by a professional and subsequent treatment. There is a greater push to make "trauma-informed practice" a standardized approach for health-care profession working with clients. This is important as the impact of trauma on patients' physical and mental health often goes undetected in therapeutic assessment/screening.

There are a number of accessible approaches used to treat PTSD. Specialized therapies such as Cognitive Behavioural Therapy (CBT), which works on correcting distorted thoughts, feelings, and behaviours, are often used in conjunction with Prolonged Exposure Therapy in order to re-establish a tolerable relationship with triggering stimuli. Another well-evidenced treatment for PTSD is Eye Movement Desensitization and Reprocessing (EMDR). Support groups and a strong support network, both formal (health-care providers) and informal (family, friends) are shown to help as well.

Diagnosis of PTSD may also result in the prescribing of psychotropic medication, e.g., Selective Serotonin Re-uptake Inhibitors (SSRI), by a family physician or psychiatrist.

In the example of PTSD and pain from motor vehicle accidents, Beck and Coffey (2007) discuss how CBT may help an MVA survivor develop positive coping skills and reframe cognitive distortions, both of which can be pain and trauma triggers. CBT can help the survivor differentiate between the circumstance of the accident and the resulting symptoms, which in turn can disrupt the triggering cycle of experiencing pain, being re-traumatized, and developing unhealthy cognitions about the accident, the pain, and themselves.

Therapy services may be offered through:
- Community mental health centres.
- Family physicians, primary care teams (nurses, alternative medicine providers).
- Community health centres (via counsellors, therapists, support groups).
- Other community services with trained counsellors/therapists.

- EAP providers (through workplace benefits).
- Spiritual leaders.

Sources for the above:

Centre for Addiction and Mental Health website.

US Department of Veterans Affairs National Center for PTSD website.

Beck & Coffey (2007), *op. cit.*

Koch (2002), *op. cit.*

Resources

Books

Bourne, Edmund J., PhD. *The Anxiety and Phobia Workbook.* 5th ed. Oakland, CA: New Harbinger Publications, 2011.

Carney, Colleen E. & Manber, Rachel, PhD. *Quiet Your Mind & Get to Sleep: Solutions to Insomnia for Those with Depression, Anxiety, or Chronic Pain.* Oakland, CA: New Harbinger Publications, 2009.

Gardner-Nix, Jackie with Costin-Hall, Lucie. *The Mindfulness Solution to Pain: Step-by-Step Techniques for Chronic Pain Management.* Oakland, CA: New Harbinger Publications, 2009.

Greenberger, Dennis, PhD, & Padesky, Christine A., PhD. *Mind Over Mood: Change How You Feel by Changing the Way You Think.* 2nd ed. Oakland, CA: New Harbinger Publications, 2015.

Hayes, Steven C., PhD, with Spencer Smith. *Get Out of Your Mind and into Your Life: The New Acceptance and Commitment Therapy.* Oakland, CA: New Harbinger Publications, 2005.

Herman, Judith L. *Trauma and Recovery: The Aftermath of Violence – from Domestic Abuse to Political Terror.* New York: Basic Books, 1997.

LeJeune, Chad, PhD. *The Worry Trap: How to Free Yourself from Worry & Anxiety Using Acceptance and Commitment Therapy.* Oakland, CA: New Harbinger Publications, 2007.

Levine, Peter A., PhD, with Frederick, Ann. *Waking the Tiger: Healing Trauma*. Berkeley, CA: North Atlantic Books, 1997.

Van der Kolk, Bessel, M.D. *The Body Keeps the Score: Brain, Mind, and Body in the Healing of Trauma*. New York: Viking, 2014.

Williams, Mark, Teasdale, John, Segal, Zindel, & Kabat-Zinn, Jon. *The Mindful Way Through Depression: Freeing Yourself from Chronic Unhappiness*. New York: Guilford Press, 2007.

Williams, Mary Beth, PhD, & Poijula, Sonia, PhD. *The PTSD Workbook: Simple, Effective Techniques for Overcoming Traumatic Stress Symptoms*. Oakland, CA: New Harbinger Publications, 2013.

Websites

Anxiety

AnxietyBC
http://www.anxietybc.com/

Anxiety Disorders Association of Canada
http://www.anxietycanada.ca/english/

Canadian Mental Health Association
https://www.cmha.ca/mental-health/
understanding-mental-illness/anxiety-disorders/

Here to Help BC
http://www.heretohelp.bc.ca/sites/default/files/images/
adtoolkit.pdf

Mood Disorders Society of Canada
https://www.mooddisorders.ca/helpful-links

Chronic Pain

The Canadian Pain Coalition
http://www.canadianpaincoalition.ca/

Chronic Pain Association of Canada
http://chronicpaincanada.com/

The Pain Toolkit
http://www.paintoolkit.org/

Depression

Centre for Addiction and Mental Health (CAMH)
http://www.camh.ca/en/hospital/health_information/a_z_
mental_health_and_addiction_information/depression/Pages/
default.aspx

Depression Hurts
http://depressionhurts.ca/en/default.aspx

Healthy Minds Canada
http://healthymindscanada.ca/resources/

Here to Help BC
http://www.heretohelp.bc.ca/factsheet/depression

Mental Health Helpline
http://www.mentalhealthhelpline.ca/

Mood Disorders Society of Canada
http://www.mooddisorderscanada.ca/

Post-traumatic Stress Disorder (PTSD)

Centre for Addiction and Mental Health (CAMH)
http://www.camh.ca/en/hospital/health_information/a_z_
mental_health_and_addiction_information/Post-traumatic/
Pages/ptsd.aspx

Gift From Within
http://www.giftfromwithin.org/html/ptsd-and-trauma-
bookstore.html

Good Therapy
http://www.goodtherapy.org/blog/best-of-2013-
goodtherapyorgs-top-10-websites-for-ptsd-trauma-1213137

National Institute of Mental Health
http://www.nimh.nih.gov/health/topics/post-traumatic-stress-
disorder-ptsd/index.shtml

PTSD Association of Canada
http://www.ptsdassociation.com/

US Department of Veterans Affairs
http://www.ptsd.va.gov/

Discussion Questions for
An Honest House

While this book is essentially a sequel to the author's memoir *A Good Home*, it is a book in its own right. It provides additional insight into the lives of Cynthia and her family over several years following a car accident.

1. Chapter two is entitled "Gone." What was actually gone? Why do you think the author chose such a title?

2. Why do you think the author was so attached to the farmhouse?

3. In many sections, the author speaks about losing her confidence. Was she being objective or was she overcome by her health issues?

4. Did the first public reading of *A Good Home* achieve its objectives for the author? Explain.

5. We hear about post-traumatic stress disorder (PTSD) as affecting persons such as war veterans and first responders to a scene of tragedy. Why did it seem to take so long before the author recognized and acknowledged that she was a victim of PTSD?

6. Throughout her struggle to deal with her pain, PTSD, and depression, the author turns to her faith in God. What is it that religion/faith offers, especially in times of need and stress?

7. Many instances of humorous exchanges are recounted between the author and her spouse, Hamlin. What does this tell us about the relationship they established in their marriage?

8. What role does humour play in helping the author cope with pain and depression?

9. How do we know that attending and participating in the Women's Conference was a courageous undertaking by the author? What did she achieve/learn from the experience?

10. Why do you think the third section of the memoir focuses primarily on the author's spouse, Hamlin?

11. Having to sell and move from the farmhouse must have been an emotional experience. Why was it necessary for Cynthia and Hamlin to do that, and what defence mechanism did the couple use to help them cope?

12. In this memoir, the author takes the reader on a very personal journey. While pain, PTSD, and depression seem ever-present, the author also shares rich family experiences and joy. What can we learn/take away from this to enrich our own lives?

CPSIA information can be obtained
at www.ICGtesting.com
Printed in the USA
LVOW04s0243130516

488013LV00010BA/31/P